Printed in the United States
By Bookmasters

T0207869

The
ANGEL
CODE
ORACLE
2020

A 12-Month Angel Journey to Activate
Your Infinite Heart

KateBeloved Levensohn

BALBOA.PRESS
A DIVISION OF HAY HOUSE

Balboa Press books may be ordered through booksellers or by contacting:

Balboa Press
A Division of Hay House
1663 Liberty Drive
Bloomington, IN 47403
www.balboapress.com
1 (877) 407-4847

Because of the dynamic nature of the Internet, any web addresses or links contained in this book may have changed since publication and may no longer be valid. The views expressed in this work are solely those of the author and do not necessarily reflect the views of the publisher, and the publisher hereby disclaims any responsibility for them.

The author of this book does not dispense medical advice or prescribe the use of any technique as a form of treatment for physical, emotional, or medical problems without the advice of a physician, either directly or indirectly. The intent of the author is only to offer information of a general nature to help you in your quest for emotional and spiritual well-being. In the event you use any of the information in this book for yourself, which is your constitutional right, the author and the publisher assume no responsibility for your actions.

Any people depicted in stock imagery provided by Getty Images are models, and such images are being used for illustrative purposes only. Certain stock imagery © Getty Images.

Print information available on the last page.

ISBN: 978-1-9822-3633-5 (sc)
ISBN: 978-1-9822-3656-4 (e)

Balboa Press rev. date: 10/24/2019

2020 is the Gateway to the Infinite Heart!

Darling Heart, I am so excited you are entering the Gateway to the Infinite Heart!

I received these Angel Code Oracle teachings in the summer of 2019 from my primary guide Archangel Ariel. Even after all these years together, I am still amazed how powerful and timely each new teaching is! These teachings are exactly what we need right now!

Abundant Angel Blessings
Beloved

ARIEL SPEAKS | PURPOSE FOR THESE TEACHINGS
Channeled Message from Archangel Ariel - July 26, 2019

Child, we are inviting you through these Angel Code Oracle teachings to expand your understanding… to bring in the Cosmic Divine Oneness… to assist others in the unification of Spirit Into Matter.

Living as Soul Beings is the only way to PEACE. Living in the knowing that ALL ARE ONE is the only way to protect your planet. Earth is a planet of free will where Soul Beings came to experience life in physical form. To enjoy Paradise… clean… pure. To create relationships, families, communities, ideas, inventions, to enjoy great abundance, vibrant health, happiness, joy and wealth all through the vibration of LOVE and the knowing that ALL ARE ONE.

Earth was a paradise… a planet of plenty. But some forgot… they put their way forward as the only way. Their God, their holy books, their skin color, their wants, their desires.

This is where your planet is now. In the hands of those who have forgotten.

It is time for remembering. It is time to return to the ancient spiritual understanding and to live only through the Infinite SoulHeart. LOVE… HONOUR… RESPECT… COMPASSION are actions of the SoulHeart.

Child, we want Humanity to awaken… It is beyond time to return to these understandings. No Child, not just understanding but living these truths.

All Are One… All Are Divine

*2020 is a turning point. As it is said on your planet "A watershed year". In these new ANGEL CODE ORACLE teachings, the year **2020 is the Gateway to the Infinite Heart**. It is time Child.*

We are complete.
End transmission.

About This Book

Blessings Darling Heart,

What you are holding in your hand is not just a 2020 diary, it's a powerful 12-month journey to activate your Infinite Heart and manifest your dreams! …And it's created with my primary guide Archangel Ariel!

Sweet One, you know you are a powerful creator who wants to create the most abundant, loving, vibrantly healthy and prosperous life! You understand the importance of working with unseen guides especially the angels and you understand the importance of using tools like numerology and astrology for energetic alignment. You'd love to have a roadmap for the year, especially one that follows the cycles of the Moon and lets you know what the energies are and how best to align with them to reach your goals.

Using THE ANGEL CODE ORACLE 2020 and the angelic guidance (Archangel Ariel's Messages), angel affirmations (Angel Mantra) astrology (Luna's Astro Energies) and numerology (Angel Codes) you can easily align your energy with the energies of nature and the cosmos. You'll know the appropriate times to create and the appropriate times to surrender! And you'll activate the cosmic support you're receiving!

Dear One, THE ANGEL CODE ORACLE 2020 serves as the perfect place for you to do your moon work! You'll learn about each Lunar Cycle. The weeks with a new or full moon list the lunar energy, astrological sign, element and archangel for that moon. Each moon you'll find pages inviting you to align with the current new or full moon cycle to create your goals, clarify and clear blocks to achieving those goals and create a three-step plan to manifest your dreams! We've even added new and full moon ceremonies!

There are so many amazing angel teachings, moon astrology teachings, and numerology teachings available, but none bring them all together in one place the way THE ANGEL CODE ORACLE 2020 does!

We are thrilled you have chosen to embark on this magical 12-Month Journey to Activate Your Infinite Heart!

As Archangel Ariel says, *"2020 is a turning point. As it is said on your planet, a watershed year. In these new ANGEL CODE ORACLE teachings, the year* **2020 is the Gateway to the Infinite Heart.***"*

May your heart be filled to overflowing and may you awaken each and every one you meet!

Abundant Angel Blessings
Beloved
The Angel Code Oracle

Ariel Speaks | About this Book

Channeled Message from Archangel Ariel - August 26, 2019

Dear One, we are most delighted you have chosen to journey with us in 2020.

2020 is the year of infinite heart and we call this journey THE ANGEL CODE ORACLE 2020; A 12-Month Journey to Activate Your Infinite Heart. In this timing upon your planet it is most important for you to awaken and align with your divine cosmic self, your soul heart... Your INFINITE HEART!

We invite you, now, to release any limiting beliefs and old ways of understanding.

Here in this book we have given you guidance to achieve alignment. We invite you to move through 2020 following the guidance within these pages. As you do, you will find yourself expressing your SoulHeart... your Infinite Heart. And as you live through your SoulHeart, your Divine Cosmic Self, you will see your life unfold in more abundance and joy.

Remember, Dear One, you are a powerful magnificent Divine Soul choosing to live life on this beautiful blue planet.

2020 is the year of the Infinite Heart... Time to surrender limitations, align your soul with the divine and create the heart-centered life of abundance, blissful love, vibrant health, and material wealth you came to Earth to experience!

We give this to you with love and blessings
We are complete.
End Transmission.

About the Angel Codes

The Angel Code Oracle is the newest teaching I have received from my primary guide, Archangel Ariel.

Based on the vibrational resonance of 13, each code 0-12 within The Angel Code Oracle is a Gateway into higher frequencies and understandings. Weaving together angel wisdom, astrology, numerology, lunar cycles and cosmic energies The Angel Code Oracle creates new tapestries of understanding… tapestries aligning with new energetic imprints infusing Spirit into Matter.

Its purpose is to bring in the Cosmic Divine Oneness… to activate your SoulHeart, assist you in the unification of Spirit into Matter and to ease your way on your Earth Journey. Remember, Dear Heart, you are a Spiritual Being experiencing life in physical form. As you align and merge your Earth Energies with your Divine Cosmic Energies you create a more delicious life of ease and grace!

We trust you will find THE ANGEL CODE ORACLE valuable along your journey.

A SHORT GLOSSARY

- Our simplified definition for Infinite Heart and SoulHeart is the place where your Soul dwells. We use Infinite Heart and SoulHeart interchangeably.
- Overlighting Angel Code is the underlying energies of a month, a moon, a day etc.
- Lunation Angel Code is the energy of the actual New or Full Moon.
- Wheel of the Year is the way we describe certain timing (equinox, solstice).

A special thank you to our amazingly meticulous editor, N. Bree Narducci for the endless hours she spent making sure you would have a fabulously clean manuscript to enjoy!

Bio

Beloved
The Angel Code Oracle

OMGoddess Darling Hearts, my journey this lifetime has been absolutely delicious. I've been blessed beyond measure and my Joy and my Passion is Activating "Sleeping" Souls.

I love sharing what I've experienced... to partner with you... assisting you to live the most joyful and abundant life you can imagine! After all, Dear One, that's why you chose your beautiful Earth body... so you can experience all the things you can only experience when you are Spirit manifesting itself into Matter!

I am often out and about playing in the Cosmos with my unseen friends, especially my primary guide Archangel Ariel! I re-awakened to the angels and Archangel Ariel almost thirty years ago and we've been teaching, writing, facilitating retreats and helping clients awaken their souls, clarify their dreams, create goals, identify and clear blocks, and create the most deliciously abundant lives they can imagine!

THE ANGEL CODE ORACLE 2020 is our newest teaching and our latest book.

If you'd like to know more, please visit our website **www.TheAngelCodeOracle.com**

The Angel Code Oracle 2020; A 12-Month Angel Journey to Activate Your Infinite Heart
is part of the Angelic Guide to Joyful Living Series.
Other titles include:
Ariel's Journey
30 Days to Prosperity and Abundance

Cosmic Happenings in 2020

Moon Dates 2020
(All Dates and Times are Us/New York)

FRIDAY, JANUARY 10
FULL MOON
PENUMBRAL LUNAR ECLIPSE

FRIDAY, JANUARY 24
NEW MOON

SUNDAY, FEBRUARY 9
FULL MOON

SUNDAY, FEBRUARY 23
NEW MOON

MONDAY, MARCH 9
FULL MOON

TUESDAY, MARCH 24
NEW MOON

TUESDAY, APRIL 7
FULL MOON

WEDNESDAY, APRIL 22
NEW MOON

THURSDAY, MAY 7
FULL MOON

FRIDAY, MAY 22
NEW MOON

FRIDAY, JUNE 5
FULL MOON
PENUMBRAL LUNAR ECLIPSE

SUNDAY, JUNE 21
NEW MOON
ANNULAR SOLAR ECLIPSE

SUNDAY, JULY 5
FULL MOON
PENUMBRAL LUNAR ECLIPSE

MONDAY, JULY 20
NEW MOON

MONDAY, AUGUST 3
FULL MOON

TUESDAY, AUGUST 18
NEW MOON

WEDNESDAY, SEPTEMBER 2
FULL MOON

THURSDAY, SEPTEMBER 17
NEW MOON

THURSDAY, OCTOBER 1
FULL MOON

FRIDAY, OCTOBER 16
NEW MOON

SATURDAY, OCTOBER 31
FULL MOON (BLUE MOON)

SUNDAY, NOVEMBER 15
NEW MOON

MONDAY, NOVEMBER 30
FULL MOON
PENUMBRAL LUNAR ECLIPSE

MONDAY, DECEMBER 14
NEW MOON
TOTAL SOLAR ECLIPSE

TUESDAY, DECEMBER 29
FULL MOON

Eclipses 2020
(All Dates and Times are Us/New York)

FRIDAY, JANUARY 10
PENUMBRAL ECLIPSE (FULL MOON)
ECLIPSE BEGINS: 12:07 PM
ECLIPSE PEAK 2:11 PM
ECLIPSE ENDS: 4:12 PM
ASTRO SIGN: 19° CANCER

FRIDAY, JUNE 5
PENUMBRAL ECLIPSE (FULL MOON)
ECLIPSE BEGINS: 1:45 PM
ECLIPSE PEAK: 3:26 PM
ECLIPSE ENDS: 5:04 PM
ASTRO SIGN: 15° SAGITTARIUS

SUNDAY, JUNE 20/21
ANNULAR SOLAR ECLIPSE (NEW MOON)
ECLIPSE BEGINS: JUNE 20 11:45 PM
ECLIPSE PEAK: JUNE 21 2:41 AM
ECLIPSE ENDS: JUNE 21 5:34 AM
ASTRO SIGN: 0° CANCER

SUNDAY, JULY 4/5
PENUMBRAL LUNAR ECLIPSE (FULL MOON)
ECLIPSE BEGINS: JULY 4 11:07 PM
ECLIPSE PEAK: JULY 5 12:31 AM
ECLIPSE ENDS: JULY 5 1:52 AM
ASTRO SIGN: 13° CAPRICORN

MONDAY, NOVEMBER 30
PENUMBRAL LUNAR ECLIPSE (FULL MOON)
ECLIPSE BEGINS: 2:32 AM
ECLIPSE PEAK: 4:44 AM
ECLIPSE ENDS: 6:53 AM New York
ASTRO SIGN: 8° GEMINI

MONDAY, DECEMBER 14
TOTAL SOLAR ECLIPSE (NEW MOON)
ECLIPSE BEGINS: 8:33 AM
ECLIPSE PEAK: 11:14 AM
ECLIPSE ENDS: 1:53 PM
ASTRO SIGN: 23° SAGITTARIUS

Equinox, Solstice, Seasons 2020
(All Dates and Times are Us/New York)

THURSDAY, MARCH 19 EQUINOX
TIME: 11:49 PM
SEASON: SPRING EQUINOX NORTH OF THE EQUATOR / AUTUMN EQUINOX SOUTH OF THE EQUATOR

SATURDAY, JUNE 20 SOLSTICE
TIME: 5:43 PM
SEASON: SUMMER NORTH OF THE EQUATOR / WINTER SOUTH OF THE EQUATOR

TUESDAY, SEPTEMBER 22 EQUINOX
TIME: 9:30 AM
SEASON: AUTUMN NORTH OF THE EQUATOR / SPRING SOUTH OF THE EQUATOR

MONDAY, DECEMBER 21 SOLSTICE
TIME: 5:02 AM
SEASON: WINTER NORTH OF THE EQUATOR / SUMMER SOUTH OF THE EQUATOR

Mercury Retrogrades 2020

(All dates and times are US/New York)

FEBRUARY 18 (AQUARIUS) – MARCH 9 (PISCES)
JUNE 19 (GEMINI) – JULY 11 (CANCER)
OCTOBER 16 (LIBRA) – NOVEMBER 2 (SCORPIO)

12-Month Journey to Activate Your Infinite Heart

January 2020 Overlighting Angel Code: 5 | Gateway of The Angelic Triangle

Activation: Activates your connection to direct angel communication through the Angelic Triangle.

* To activate The Angelic Triangle, place your thumbs on your throat and your fingers on your ears. Do you feel the Triangle? Be still. Is there a Truth you need to speak? Is there a message you need to hear?

How delicious! The first month of our new year begins with the Overlighting Angel Code of Angel Connection aligned with 5 | Gateway of the Angelic Triangle. The Angels are inviting you into this beautiful new year with angels as your partners! They're reminding you that they are always with you but since you live on a planet of free will, you must invite them into your life as playmates, partners and guides!

ARCHANGEL ARIEL'S MESSAGE 5 | GATEWAY OF THE ANGELIC TRIANGLE

Yes. As Little One has said, you are invited here to deepen your relationship with your angels. Nurture your relationship with your angels the way you nurture your relationship with your best friend. Do you call your best friend to chat or visit … sharing the happenings of your life … asking for advice or opinions when needed?

Would you miss your friend if time was long between visits? And yet when once again you meet, is it not as though no time has elapsed? Do you know each other so well that the passage of time makes no difference? And yet, Dear One, does it not make your life sweeter, more fragrant, more delicious to have long chats, share secrets, and enjoy tea together? This is how it is with your angels. We are ever present, and your angels know you can get busy with life in the third dimension and sometimes you might forget to invite your angels. Dear One, life is so much sweeter and more fragrant when you have long chats, share secrets and enjoy life in the company of angels!

Each morning when you awaken from slumber invite your angels to play with you!

JANUARY ANGEL MANTRA

🦋 *"Angels are waiting for my invitation to join me as partners, playmates and guides. All I have to do is ask!"*

THIS MONTH'S ANGEL MANTRA ACTIVATION

Each morning this month look into a mirror and begin taking long, slow, deep breaths all the way into your belly. As you breathe, bring your awareness into your SoulHeart. Feel your beautiful SoulHeart expanding. Feel the shift. Do you feel warm … or cool? Do you feel vibration? See color? Now, bring your awareness back to your breath and take 3 long, slow, deep breaths. On each outbreath, repeat or tone the Angel Mantra out loud:

🦋 *"Angels are waiting for my invitation to join me as partners, playmates and guides. All I have to do is ask!"*

Repeat for a total of 3 breaths. For an even deeper alignment, repeat this in the evenings, too!

Our FREE Thank You Gift for You!

We've created 2 amazing video gifts to help you make 2020 an absolutely deliciously magical year! To receive your FREE videos, please e-mail us at the e-mail address below and we'll send your free videos directly to your inbox!

🦋 How-To Use Angel Code Oracle 2020
   To receive this video please send your e-mail to:
   Taco2020How-To@katebeloved.com
🦋 3-Video Angel Code Masterclass
   To receive this video please send your e-mail to:
   Taco2020MasterClass@katebeloved.com

Wishing you an absolutely delicious 2020!

Abundant Angel Blessings
Beloved

january

SUNDAY	MONDAY	TUESDAY
5	6	7
12	13	14
19	20	21
26	27	28

2020

WEDNESDAY	THURSDAY	FRIDAY	SATURDAY
1	2	3	4
8	9	10 FULL MOON ECLIPSE (CANCER) ANGEL CODES: 6/10	11
15	16	17	18
22	23	24 NEW MOON (AQUARIUS) ANGEL CODES: 11/4	25
29	30	31	

JAN

january

S	M	T	W	T	F	S
			1	2	3	4
5	6	7	8	9	10	11
12	13	14	15	16	17	18
19	20	21	22	23	24	25
26	27	28	29	30	31	

notes

30 MONDAY	31 TUESDAY	1 WEDNESDAY

	2 THURSDAY	3 FRIDAY	4 SATURDAY	5 SUNDAY

January Full Moon Lunar Eclipse

DATE: FRIDAY, JANUARY 10 / LUNATION: 12:23 PM (NEW YORK)
ASTRO SIGN: 19° CANCER / RULER: MOON
ELEMENT: WATER / EXPRESSION: CARDINAL
ARCHANGEL: RAPHAEL

FULL MOON KEYWORDS: COMPLETION, SURRENDER

ECLIPSES

Oh My! Our first eclipse of the year. This is a penumbral eclipse. Eclipses usually come in pairs and activate a particular axis (astrological signs that are opposite each other). This eclipse in Cancer activates the Cancer/Capricorn Axis. Eclipses amplify the lunar energies about three times more than a non-eclipse moon!

LUNA'S ASTRO ENERGIES

When Lady Luna is shining her Cancerian light, she is highlighting home and family. I invite you to tune into your Infinite Heart. Where does your beautiful Infinite Heart, your SoulHeart, feel "at home"? Who is your Heart family?

JANUARY 10 CANCER FULL MOON ANGEL CODE 6/10

Friday's Full Moon Eclipse at 19° Cancer activates the ANGEL CODE 6/10 shining the light of the Universal Light Star into your God's Eye, awakening your Infinite Knowing!

OVERLIGHTING ANGEL CODE 6 | GATEWAY OF INFINITE KNOWING
Activation: Activates your intuition in all realms and dimensions.

Darling Heart, this Angel Code activates your Infinite Knowing! The angels are reminding you that you are a magnificent Spirit Being experiencing a life in matter. You came to earth to experience a life on the material plane, yet you are a very powerful intuitive! You are one with the Universe and all can be known. Intuitive knowing is one of your many gifts of spirit! Remember, Dear Heart, you are a Master Intuitive.

ARCHANGEL ARIEL'S MESSAGE 6 | GATEWAY OF INFINITE KNOWING

Dear One, remember you are a masterful intuitive being. You are not of the earth. Yes, part of your being is in your Earth Body …. Yet, there is so much more to you. You are a multi- dimensional cosmic being and as such you may know and understand many dimensions and unseen realms. You are a masterful Intuitive and as you awaken you will tune into the Infinite Knowing …. Through the Eye of God! Unexpected knowings at first and then skill to tune in when you are wanting information. Synchronicities are your validation of opening God's Eye of Infinite Knowing. The more synchronicities you notice in your life, the more you understand your God's Eye is indeed opening! Remember too, Dear One, you are one with the universe and all can be known!

ANGEL CODE 10 | GATEWAY OF THE UNIVERSAL LIGHT STAR
Activation: Activates Light unifying your physical Body Temple with your Light Body, Divine Light of the Universe and all Benevolent Light Beings.

The Angels are reminding you that you are a Light Being living in a physical human body. Here, they connect you to the Divine Light of the Universe and all Light Beings as they align your physical body with your Light Body. Do not hide your Light beneath the barrel… Shine Bright Dear One! And, this code is amplified because both sun and moon and day are activating the 10!

ARCHANGEL ARIEL'S MESSAGE 10 | GATEWAY OF THE UNIVERSAL LIGHT STAR

Dear One, Angel Code 10 brings light from the universe into your physical body. Light holds the divine spark… light is energy. Energy of the universe is pouring through your physical body temple bringing spirit into matter… illuminating you with Divine Grace! Share your Light! Shine bright for all to see!

JANUARY 10 CANCER FULL MOON ACTIVATION FOR LOVE

Full Moons activate completion and surrendering things in your life that no longer serve a purpose. And, of course, Sweet One, always surrender with love and gratitude.

How divinely delicious! This first moon of 2020 the YEAR OF THE INFINITE HEART is a full moon with the powerful support of Archangel Raphael and Lady Luna in her Cancerian energies, offering you an opportunity to go into your Infinite Heart and surrender blocks to love in your life!

Please take some quiet time this week feeling into the Angel Codes **6 | Gateway of Infinite Knowing** and **10 | Gateway of The Universal Light Star**. Feel into **Lady Luna's Astro Energies of Moon ruled Cancer**. Here Luna is in her watery native energies. She rules the tides and your emotions! She rules home and family. How can you use these energies to help you surrender blocks to LOVE?

Darling Heart, we invite you to spend some quiet time on Friday tuning into your beautiful Infinite Heart, feeling into your dreams and wishes. Feeling into Love. On this full moon decide on one thing you want to surrender that you believe is keeping your Heart from experiencing its most delicious Joy. To help you sort it out, call on Archangel Raphael, Angel of Cancer, Angel of the Heart, Angel of Love, Healing and Forgiveness. For this first Full Moon of the year let's focus on your beautiful Self! Here are some things to ask yourself:

What is your passion? _____
_____

What makes your heart sing? _____
_____

Do you have a BFF? __ yes __no If you checked no, what is keeping you from this deep friendship?
_____
_____

Are you in a meaningful relationship? yes __no__ If you checked no, what is keeping you from a meaningful relationship?
_____
_____

Are you close to your family? yes __ no__ If you checked no, what is keeping you from a close family relationship?
_____
_____

Do you love yourself? yes __no__ If you checked no, what is keeping you from absolutely adoring your totally awesome self?
_____

Are you nourishing yourself? yes __ no__ If you checked no, what is keeping you from nourishing your beautiful Self?
_____
_____

Do you feel good about who you are? yes __no__ If you checked no, what don't you feel good about?
_____
_____

Look at what you've written and create one thing you are willing to surrender that you believe blocks LOVE in your life.

_____

_____

JANUARY 10 CANCER FULL MOON FIRE CEREMONY OF SURRENDER

Gather Your Sacred Tools:

- The Angel Code Oracle 2020
- A candle and lighter
- A fireproof bowl
- A small piece of paper for burning
- A pen or pencil

Go to a space where you won't be disturbed and light your candle. Call in Archangel Raphael to help you come fully into your shining heart as you release with love and gratitude. Write whatever you are surrendering on a small slip of paper. Read what you've written out loud. You might use these words.

"By the light of this full moon I surrender _____to the Sacred Fires. I surrender with Love and Gratitude and I am now complete with _____."

Then light your paper and watch it burn. Knowing you have surrendered, released and are now complete. Sit for a moment. Feel into the power of surrender. And now write whatever impressions, feelings, awareness you have.

_____

_____

_____

_____

Thank Archangel Raphael and Lady Luna and extinguish your fire.

What to do with the ashes? Many people choose to bury them. I like to go outside by the light of the moon, hold the ashes in my palm and blow them away!

Darling Heart, a surrendering ceremony is really powerful … trust that whatever you have released no longer has power over you and be sure not to re-invoke it into your life!

JAN

january

S	M	T	W	T	F	S
			1	2	3	4
5	6	7	8	9	10	11
12	13	14	15	16	17	18
19	20	21	22	23	24	25
26	27	28	29	30	31	

notes

6 MONDAY	7 TUESDAY	8 WEDNESDAY

9 THURSDAY	**10** FRIDAY	**11** SATURDAY	**12** SUNDAY
	FULL MOON *PENUMBRAL LUNAR ECLIPSE* ASTRO SIGN: CANCER ANGEL CODES: 6/10		

JAN

january

S	M	T	W	T	F	S
			1	2	3	4
5	6	7	8	9	10	11
12	13	14	15	16	17	18
19	20	21	22	23	24	25
26	27	28	29	30	31	

notes

13 MONDAY	**14** TUESDAY	**15** WEDNESDAY

16 THURSDAY	**17** FRIDAY	**18** SATURDAY	**19** SUNDAY

January New Moon

DATE: FRIDAY, JANUARY 24 / LUNATION: 2:44 PM (NEW YORK)
ASTRO SIGN: 4° AQUARIUS / RULER: SATURN
ELEMENT: AIR / EXPRESSION: FIXED
ARCHANGEL: GABRIEL

NEW MOON KEYWORDS: NEW BEGINNINGS, CREATION

LUNA'S ASTRO ENERGIES

When Luna is activating Saturn/Uranus ruled Aquarian energies, she is inviting you inward to play. Become the observer. Observe with all of your senses. Become the humanitarian. How can you make this world a better place?

JANUARY 24 AQUARIUS NEW MOON ANGEL CODE 11/4

OVERLIGHTING ANGEL CODE 11 | GATEWAY TO THE GALAXIES
Activation: Activates your expansion of consciousness to travel beyond time and space.

This Angel code invites you to expand your consciousness, surrender limitations and journey beyond time and space. Angels invite you to understand clocks are an agreement made by society to keep things running smoothly in the everyday … Angels invite you to play with time and space. Stay fully present in the moment in that place of no time and no space. Stay in the knowing that there is no time nor space beyond the present.

ARCHANGEL ARIEL'S MESSAGE 11 | GATEWAY TO THE GALAXIES

And so, Dear One, here we have the activation of the code 11 the Galactic Gateway. Dear One, you are a limitless being. Your natural state of being knows no boundaries … Knows no clocks … No shoulds … No color within the lines. There is limitless freedom as you allow yourself to experience your Galactic self! Sing … Dance … Drum … Jump timelines! As was written in an earth song "We are Stardust" and so you are.

LUNATION ANGEL CODE 4 | GATEWAY TO THE INFINITE HEART
Activation: Activating your Light of Infinite Love shining through your Infinite SoulHeart.

The angels are reminding you that you are a Being of Infinite Love shining through your Infinite SoulHeart. And, this code is amplified because both sun and moon are activating the 4!

ARCHANGEL ARIEL'S MESSAGE 4 | GATEWAY TO THE INFINITE HEART

Remember Dear One, you are a divine being choosing a life in the physical form. It is your infinite SoulHeart that is meant to guide you. For you are meant to live on your planet as a divine being experiencing the most delicious life you can imagine. Remember, Dear One, only a portion of your divine being is within your physical form. You have many waiting to serve you. Angels, guides, ascended masters, cosmic beings... your connection to all of your soul gifts and talents is through your magnificent heart. Let your heart be your guide. When things feel resonant move forward. When you are feeling discord, retreat. Allow your awareness of your SoulHeart frequency to grow. When you are not sure, feel into your Infinite SoulHeart. Ask questions. Feel into your heart. You will become more skilled as you practice.

JANUARY 24 AQUARIUS NEW MOON ACTIVATION FOR LOVE

New Moons activate new beginnings, visioning, setting goals and creating! You now have the powerful support of Archangel Gabriel and Lady Luna in her Aquarian energies. As we move through the Wheel of the Year, this first New Moon invites you to focus on creating more LOVE in your life!

Please take some quiet time this week feeling into the **Angel Codes 11 | Gateway To The Galaxies** and **4 | Gateway To The Infinite Heart.** Feel into **Lady Luna's Astro Energies of Saturn and Uranus ruled Aquarius.** Here airy Luna is flying through the Cosmos chatting with everyone she meets... she creates through communication. She creates balance, beauty and love! How can these energies help you activate more Love?

Darling Heart, we invite you to spend some quiet time on Friday tuning into your beautiful Infinite Heart, feeling into your dreams and wishes. Feeling in to Love. Call on Archangel Gabriel, Angel of Aquarius, Angel of Inspiration and Divine Communication to partner with you as you tune in to expressions of LOVE!

And now, Sweet One, ask yourself the following questions:

What is your passion? _____
_____

What makes your heart sing?_____
_____

What are your favorite ways of expressing romantic love in your life?
    writing___ art___ talking ___ singing ___ dancing _ touching ___ eye gazing___ sex___
    other_____

What are your favorite ways of expressing non-romantic love in your life?
    writing___ art___ talking ___ singing ___ dancing _ touching ___ eye gazing___
    other _____

How can you bring more of that into your life during this Lunar cycle?

_____
_____
_____

From the questions above write down 3 dreams you'd like to create to bring more LOVE into your life.

_____
_____
_____

Read each dream out loud. Feel into it. Does one stand out from the other two? Does one bring a smile as you read it? Is one easier to manifest? Or do you feel the timing is right … Or not?

Which dream on your list of 3 is the one to activate during this lunar cycle?

_____
_____

JANUARY 24 AQUARIUS NEW MOON CEREMONY OF CREATION

Gather Your Sacred Tools:

- The Angel Code Oracle 2020
- A candle and lighter
- Paper, pens, markers etc.
- A pen or pencil

Sweet One, go to a space where you won't be disturbed and light your candle. Call in Archangel Gabriel to help inspire you as you come fully into your shining heart preparing to activate your New Moon dream! Allow yourself plenty of time to play with this!

Review the dream you decided to activate during this lunar cycle and write a creation statement (an intention) to create more LOVE into your life. Remember your statement is to be in the present and not in the future!

_____
_____

OK, Dear Heart, now let's turn that intention into a goal with 3 actionable steps!

3 actions I am taking in the next two weeks to manifest my intention to bring more delicious LOVE into my life!

_____

_____

_____

_____

Awesome! You now have a goal and 3 actionable steps to take!

Here's the next part of your New Moon Creation Ceremony! We invite you to create a mini angel board! It's a vision board with the Angels! On your paper using your pens and markers write your intention and the 3 actions you are taking in the next two weeks!

Be sure to write Thank You on your board. You can write a simple Thank You or something more elaborate, "Thank You Angels and Lady Luna for this and all deliciousness I'm creating now!"

Be creative! Create something you'd like to look at least once a day, each and EVERY day! Make it fun ... catchy ... playful!!

When you've completed your mini angel, board put your tools away.

Thank Archangel Gabriel and Lady Luna and extinguish your candle.

Be sure to place your Angel Board where you will see it every day for the next two weeks!

Here are some things you might like to do to keep your mini angel board in your awareness:

- Take a picture on your phone and make it your screen saver.
- Take a photo on your computer and make it your screen saver.
- Frame it and put it on your desk or in your kitchen.
- Keep it on your bed stand. It's great seeing it first thing in the morning and again, just before falling asleep!

Dear Heart, FOLLOW YOUR ACTIONABLE STEPS! When you DO something toward your goals you are actually creating an energetic alignment. And you know alignment helps you manifest more quickly!

JAN

january

S	M	T	W	T	F	S
			1	2	3	4
5	6	7	8	9	10	11
12	13	14	15	16	17	18
19	20	21	22	23	24	25
26	27	28	29	30	31	

notes

20 MONDAY	21 TUESDAY	22 WEDNESDAY

23 THURSDAY	24 FRIDAY	25 SATURDAY	26 SUNDAY
	NEW MOON ASTRO SIGN: AQUARIUS ANGEL CODES: 11/4		

JAN

january

S	M	T	W	T	F	S
			1	2	3	4
5	6	7	8	9	10	11
12	13	14	15	16	17	18
19	20	21	22	23	24	25
26	27	28	29	30	31	

notes

27 MONDAY	28 TUESDAY	29 WEDNESDAY

30	**31**	**1**	**2**
THURSDAY	FRIDAY	SATURDAY	SUNDAY

February 2020 Overlighting Angel Code
6 | Gateway of Infinite Knowing

Activation: Activates your intuition in all realms and dimensions.

The Overlighting Angel Code for February 2020 is 6 | GATEWAY OF INFINITE KNOWING. Darling Heart, you came to earth to experience a life on the material plane, yet you are a very powerful intuitive! Intuitive knowing is one of your many gifts of spirit! This month, you're invited to reawaken your infinite knowing. The Angels are reminding you that you are a magnificent Spirit Being experiencing a life in matter. You are one with the Universe and all can be known. Remember, Dear Heart, you are a Master Intuitive.

ARCHANGEL ARIEL'S MESSAGE 6 | GATEWAY OF INFINITE KNOWING

Dear One, remember you are a masterful intuitive being. You are not of the Earth. Yes, part of your being is in your Earth Body. Yet, there is so much more to you. You are a multi- dimensional cosmic being and as such you may know and understand many dimensions and unseen realms. You are a masterful Intuitive and as you awaken you will tune into the Infinite Knowing … Through the Eye of God! Unexpected knowings at first and then skill to tune in when you are wanting information. Synchronicities are your validation of opening God's Eye of Infinite Knowing. The more synchronicities you notice in your life, the more you understand your God's Eye is indeed opening! Remember too, Dear One, you are one with the universe and all can be known!

FEBRUARY ANGEL MANTRA

🦋 *"I am a masterful intuitive. The more I follow my intuition the more perfectly I align with my inner guidance system. I am a masterful intuitive."*

THIS MONTH'S ANGEL MANTRA ACTIVATION

Each morning this month look into a mirror, begin taking long, slow, deep breaths all the way into your belly. As you breathe bring your awareness into your SoulHeart. Feel your beautiful SoulHeart expanding. Feel the shift. Do you feel warm… or cool? Do you feel vibration? See color? Now, bring your awareness back to your breath and take 3 long, slow, deep breaths. On each outbreath, repeat or tone the Angel Mantra out loud.

- *"I am a masterful intuitive. The more I follow my intuition the more perfectly I align with my inner guidance system. I am a masterful intuitive."*

Repeat for a total of 3 breaths. For an even deeper alignment, repeat this in the evenings too!

Our FREE Thank You Gift for You!

We've created 2 amazing video gifts to help you make 2020 an absolutely deliciously magical year! To receive your FREE videos, please e-mail us at the e-mail address below and we'll send your free videos directly to your inbox!

- How-To Use Angel Code Oracle 2020
  To receive this video please send your e-mail to:
  Taco2020How-To@katebeloved.com
- 3-Video Angel Code Masterclass
  To receive this video please send your e-mail to:
  Taco2020MasterClass@katebeloved.com

Wishing you an absolutely delicious 2020!

Abundant Angel Blessings
Beloved

---

february

SUNDAY	MONDAY	TUESDAY
2	3	4
9 FULL MOON (LEO) ANGEL CODES: 6/2	10	11
16	17	18 MERCURY RETROGRADE
23 NEW MOON (PISCES) ANGEL CODES: 1/4	24	25

2020

WEDNESDAY	THURSDAY	FRIDAY	SATURDAY
			1
5	6	7	8
12	13	14	15
19	20	21	22
26	27	28	29

February Full Moon

DATE: SUNDAY, FEBRUARY 9 / LUNATION: 12:34 AM (NEW YORK)
ASTRO SIGN: 20° LEO / RULER: SUN
ELEMENT: FIRE / EXPRESSION: FIXED
ARCHANGEL: URIEL

FULL MOON KEYWORDS: COMPLETION, SURRENDER

LUNA'S ASTRO ENERGIES

When Lady Luna shines her light on Sun ruled Leo, she basks in her moonlight as it activates her passion for life! Lady Luna is firmly rooted in her warm-hearted generosity! This lioness knows how to be the benevolent Queen! Lady Luna is inviting you to ignite your passion and your warm-hearted generosity as you bestow benevolent grace on all you meet.

FEBRUARY 9 LEO FULL MOON ANGEL CODE 6/2

OVERLIGHTING ANGEL CODE 6 | GATEWAY OF INFINITE KNOWING
Activation: Activates your intuition in all realms and dimensions.

You came to earth to experience life on the material plane, yet you are a very powerful intuitive! Intuitive knowing is one of your many gifts of spirit! This month you're invited to reawaken your infinite knowing. The Angels are reminding you; you are a magnificent Spirit Being experiencing a life in matter. You are one with the Universe and all can be known. Remember, Dear Heart, you are a Master Intuitive.

Darling Heart, we are called to pay attention! This Angel Code is amplified THREE times! Angel Code 6 was part of last month's Full Moon Code, it is the Overlighting Angel Code for this month AND it is part of the Angel Code for this February Full Moon!

ARCHANGEL ARIEL'S MESSAGE 6 | GATEWAY OF INFINITE KNOWING

Dear One, remember you are a masterful intuitive being. You are not of the Earth. Yes, part of your being is in your Earth Body.… Yet, there is so much more to you. You are a multi- dimensional cosmic being and as such you may know and understand many dimensions and unseen realms. You are a masterful Intuitive and as you awaken you will tune into the Infinite Knowing…. Through the Eye of God! Unexpected knowings at first and then skill to tune in when you are wanting information. Synchronicities are your validation of opening God's Eye of Infinite Knowing. The more synchronicities you notice in your life, the more you understand your God's Eye is indeed opening! Remember too, Dear One, you are one with the universe and all can be known!

LUNATION ANGEL CODE 2 | GATEWAY TO THE SACRED WOMB
Activation: Activates the creation of physical form through the sacred union of Divine Male and Divine Female.

This powerful code activates the energetic signature of Sacred Union as it unites Divine Female with Divine Male. And this Code is amplified because both the Sun and Moon are activating 2.

ARCHANGEL ARIEL'S MESSAGE 2 | GATEWAY TO THE SACRED WOMB

Dear One, the Angel Code for this lunation is quite powerful in its amplification. At this Full Moon as Luna shines her Light through Leo, you are invited to come into your Sacred Womb. A place of balance. A place of Harmony. The place where Divine Male and Divine Female are United. What will you surrender? What is complete in your Life? How will you assist your Sacred Womb to release now so at the coming New Moon you can prepare for a re-birth?

FEBRUARY 9 LEO FULL MOON ACTIVATION FOR VIBRANT HEALTH

Full Moons activate completion and surrendering things in your life that no longer serve a purpose. And, of course, Sweet One, always surrender with love and gratitude. You now have the powerful support of Archangel Uriel and Lady Luna in her Leo energies. We are inviting you, this Full Moon, to surrender habits and choices that block your Vibrant Health! And, of course, Sweet One, Vibrant Health is more than physical well-being! It's your whole self… mind… body… and soul!

Please take some quiet time this week feeling into the **Angel Codes 6 | Gateway of Infinite Knowing** and **2 | Gateway to The Sacred Womb.** Feel into **Lady Luna's Astro Energies of Sun ruled Leo.** Here Lady Luna in her fiery Leo energies lights her fires of action! You know that expression, "Put a fire under it!" Lady Lion is calling you to do just that! Here's your Call to Action! How can you use these energies to help you surrender blocks to VIBRANT HEALTH?

Darling Heart, we invite you to spend some quiet time on Sunday tuning into your beautiful Infinite Heart, feeling into your dreams and wishes. Feeling into your HEALTH. On this Full Moon decide on one thing you want to surrender that you believe is keeping you from experiencing your most perfect

Vibrant Health. To help you sort it out, call on Archangel Uriel, Angel of Leo, Angel of Light and Clarity to help you clarify what you are surrendering. Here's our simple checklist:

On a scale of 1 – 10, what's your number? _____
(10 is absolutely perfect vibrant health, 1 is being treated for illness.)

Darling Heart here are some things to consider:

How often are you moving your body? (yoga, tai chi, qigong, running, walking, gym exercise, etc.)
     1x week____ 3x week_____ More than 3x week_____ I'm inconsistent_____ Not at all _____
Are you eating foods to keep you vibrant? yes ____ no__
Are you underweight? ____ Overweight? _____
Do you meditate? 1x week____ 3x week____ More than 3x week__ I'm inconsistent__
     Not at all __
Are you sleeping well? yes ____ no __ Sometimes _____
How much time do you spend on your screen/devices daily? minutes _____hours___
Are you balancing work and play/family/friends? yes_____ no _____
Are you leaking energy by holding on to anger, blame, disappointment or loss?
     yes__ no_____
Are you holding on to guilt? yes_____ no_____

Look at what you've written and name one thing you are willing to surrender this Full Moon that you believe blocks your Vibrant Health.

_____

FEBRUARY 9 LEO FULL MOON FIRE CEREMONY OF SURRENDER

Gather Your Sacred Tools:

- The Angel Code Oracle 2020
- A candle and lighter
- A fireproof bowl
- A small piece of paper for burning
- A pen or pencil

Go to a space where you won't be disturbed and light your candle. Call in Archangel Uriel to help you come fully into your shining heart as you release with love and gratitude. Write whatever you are surrendering on a small slip of paper. Read what you've written out loud. You might use these words:

"By the light of this full moon I surrender _____ to the Sacred Fires. I surrender with Love and Gratitude and I am now complete with _____."

Then light your paper and watch it burn. Knowing you have surrendered, released and are now complete. Sit for a moment. Feel into the power of surrender. And now write whatever impressions, feelings, and awareness you have. _____

_____

_____

_____

Thank Archangel Uriel and Lady Luna and extinguish your fire.

What to do with the ashes? Many people choose to bury them. I like to go outside by the light of the moon, hold the ashes in my palm and blow them away!

Darling Heart, a surrendering ceremony is really powerful…trust that whatever you have released no longer has power over you and be sure not to re-invoke it into your life!

FEB
february

S	M	T	W	T	F	S
						1
2	3	4	5	6	7	8
9	10	11	12	13	14	15
16	17	18	19	20	21	22
23	24	25	26	27	28	29

notes

3 MONDAY	**4** TUESDAY	**5** WEDNESDAY

6 THURSDAY	7 FRIDAY	8 SATURDAY	9 SUNDAY
			FULL MOON ASTRO SIGN: LEO ANGEL CODES: 6/2

FEB

february

S	M	T	W	T	F	S
						1
2	3	4	5	6	7	8
9	10	11	12	13	14	15
16	17	18	19	20	21	22
23	24	25	26	27	28	29

notes

10 MONDAY	11 TUESDAY	12 WEDNESDAY

13
THURSDAY

14
FRIDAY

15
SATURDAY

16
SUNDAY

February New Moon

DATE: SUNDAY, FEBRUARY 23 / LUNATION 8:33 AM NEW YORK.
ASTRO SIGN: 4° PISCES / RULER: JUPITER, NEPTUNE
ELEMENT: WATER / EXPRESSION: MUTABLE
ARCHANGEL: RAPHAEL

NEW MOON KEYWORDS: NEW BEGINNING, CREATION

LUNA'S ASTRO ENERGIES

Although like Mermaid Pisces you may be swimming to your own rhythm, Lady Luna invites you not to get lost in your own watery paradise but to step into the wisdom of your intuition and create your dreams from that place of Inner Knowing. When you find darkness, shine your powerful, non-judgmental, forgiving compassion into the darkness.

FEBRUARY 23 PISCES NEW MOON ANGEL CODE 11/4

OVERLIGHTING ANGEL CODE 11 | GATEWAY TO THE GALAXIES
Activation: Activates your expansion of consciousness to travel beyond time and space.

This Angel code invites you to expand your consciousness, surrender limitations, and journey beyond time and space. Angels invite you to understand clocks are an agreement made by society to keep things running smoothly in the everyday … Angels invite you to play with time and space. Stay fully present in the moment in that place of no time and no space. Stay in the knowing that there is no time nor space beyond the present.

ARCHANGEL ARIEL'S MESSAGE 11 | GATEWAY TO THE GALAXIES

Dear One, you are a limitless being. Your natural state of being knows no boundaries … Knows no clocks … No shoulds … No color within the lines. There is limitless freedom as you allow yourself to experience your Galactic self! Sing … Dance … Drum … Jump timelines! As was written in an earth song "We are Stardust" and so you are.

LUNATION ANGEL CODE 4 | GATEWAY TO THE INFINITE HEART
Activation: Activating your Light of Infinite Love shining through your Infinite SoulHeart.

The angels are reminding you that you are a Being of Infinite Love shining through your Infinite SoulHeart. And this Code is amplified because both the Sun and Moon are activating the 4! And the ANGEL CODE for 2020 is 4!

ARCHANGEL ARIEL'S MESSAGE 4 | GATEWAY TO THE INFINITE HEART

Remember Dear One, you are a divine being choosing a life in the physical form. It is your infinite SoulHeart that is meant to guide you. For you are meant to live on your planet as a divine being experiencing the most delicious life you can imagine. Remember Dear One, only a portion of your divine being is within your physical form. You have many waiting to serve you ... Angels, guides, ascended masters, cosmic beings. Your connection to all of your soul gifts and talents is through your magnificent heart. Let your heart be your guide. When things feel resonant, move forward. When you are feeling discord, retreat. Allow your awareness of your SoulHeart frequency to grow. When you are not sure, feel into your Infinite SoulHeart. Ask questions. Feel into your heart. You will become more skilled as you practice.

FEBRUARY 23 PISCES NEW MOON ACTIVATION FOR VIBRANT HEALTH

New Moon activates new beginnings, visioning, setting goals and creating while you have powerful support of Archangel Raphael and Lady Luna. As we move through the Wheel of the Year, this New Moon is the first New Moon inviting you to uplevel your VIBRANT HEALTH! And, of course, Sweet One, VIBRANT HEALTH is more than physical well-being! It's your whole self ... mind ... body ... and soul!

Please take some quiet time this week feeling into the **Angel Codes 11 | Gateway to The Galaxies and 4 | Gateway to The Infinite Heart**. Feel into **Lady Luna's Astro Energies of Neptune/Jupiter ruled Pisces**. Here Luna is in her Watery Deep Soul. She longs to come into Oneness. How can these energies help you activate more VIBRANT HEALTH?

Darling Heart, we invite you to spend some quiet time on Sunday tuning into your beautiful Infinite Heart, feeling into your dreams and wishes around your Health. Call on Archangel Raphael, Angel of Pisces, Angel of Healing, Love and Forgiveness to help you as you create more VIBRANT HEALTH!

Sweet One, ask yourself the following question:

On a scale of 1 – 10 what's your number? _____
(10 is absolutely perfect vibrant health, 1 is being treated for illness)

And now, come to stillness and feel into your relationship with Your Health. Here are some common questions associated with Health. Check those that apply:

How often are you moving your body? (yoga, tai chi, qigong, running, walking, gym exercise, etc.)
   1x week____ 3x week____ More than 3x week_____ I'm inconsistent____ not at all _____
Are you eating foods to keep you vibrant? ____ yes ____ no
Are you underweight? ____ Overweight? _____
Do you meditate? 1x week____ 3x week__ More than 3x week__ I'm inconsistent__ Not at all __
Are you sleeping well? yes ____ no __ sometimes _____
How much time do you spend on your screen/devices daily? minutes __ hours __
Are you balancing work and play/family/friends? yes __ no __
Are you leaking energy by holding on to anger, blame, disappointment or loss? yes ____ no____
Are you holding on to guilt? yes ____ no__

From the questions above write down 3 possibilities where you can create more VIBRANT HEALTH.

_____
_____
_____

Read each possibility out loud. Feel into them. Does one stand out from the other two? Does one bring a smile as you read it? Is one easier to manifest? Do you feel the timing is right…? Or not?

Which possibility on your list of three is the one to activate during this lunar cycle?

_____
_____

FEBRUARY 23 PISCES NEW MOON CEREMONY OF CREATION

Gather Your Sacred Tools:

- 🦋 The Angel Code Oracle 2020
- 🦋 A candle and lighter
- 🦋 Paper, pens, markers etc.
- 🦋 A pen or pencil

Sweet One, go to a space where you won't be disturbed and light your candle. Call in Archangel Raphael to help inspire you as you come fully into your shining heart preparing to activate your New Moon dream! Allow yourself plenty of time to play with this!

Review the possibility you decided to activate during this lunar cycle and write a creation statement (an intention) to create more VIBRANT HEALTH. Remember your statement is to be in the present and not in the future!

_____

OK, Dear Heart, now let's turn that intention into a goal with 3 actionable steps!

3 actions I am taking in the next two weeks to create more VIBRANT HEALTH!

_____
_____
_____

Awesome! You now have a goal and 3 actionable steps to take!

Here's the next part of your New Moon Creation Ceremony! We invite you to create a mini angel board! It's a vision board with the Angels! On your paper using your pens and markers write your intention and the 3 actions you are taking in the next two weeks!

Be sure to write Thank You on your board. You can write a simple Thank You or something more elaborate, "Thank You Angels and Lady Luna for this and all deliciousness I'm creating now!"

Be creative! Create something you'd like to look at least once a day, each and EVERY day! Make it fun ... catchy ... playful!!

When you've completed your mini angel board put your tools away.

Thank Archangel Raphael and Lady Luna and extinguish your candle.

Be sure to place your Angel Board where you will see it every day for the next two weeks!
Here are some things you might like to do to keep your mini angel board in your awareness:

- Take a picture on your phone and make it your screen saver.
- Take a photo on your computer and make it your screen saver.
- Frame it and put it on your desk or in your kitchen.
- Keep it on your bed stand. It's great seeing it first thing in the morning and again, just before falling asleep!

Dear Heart, FOLLOW YOUR ACTIONABLE STEPS! When you DO something toward your goals you are actually creating an energetic alignment. And you know alignment helps you manifest more quickly!

FEB

february

S	M	T	W	T	F	S
						1
2	3	4	5	6	7	8
9	10	11	12	13	14	15
16	17	18	19	20	21	22
23	24	25	26	27	28	29

notes

17 MONDAY	**18** TUESDAY	**19** WEDNESDAY
	MERCURY RETROGRADE	

20 THURSDAY	21 FRIDAY	22 SATURDAY	23 SUNDAY
			NEW MOON ASTRO SIGN: PISCES ANGEL CODES: 1/4

FEB
february

S	M	T	W	T	F	S
						1
2	3	4	5	6	7	8
9	10	11	12	13	14	15
16	17	18	19	20	21	22
23	24	25	26	27	28	29

notes

24 MONDAY	25 TUESDAY	26 WEDNESDAY

27 THURSDAY	28 FRIDAY	29 SATURDAY	1 SUNDAY

March 2020 Overlighting Angel Code
7 | Gateway to The Divine Collective

Activation: Activates your connection to the Collective Consciousness.

March brings us the Overlighting Angel Code 7, the energetic signature of the Collective Consciousness! Here, you are reminded that you are a being of Divine Energy. You are part of the Divine Collective. Your thoughts and actions are energy forms that affect the whole of life... even the weather!

ARCHANGEL ARIEL'S MESSAGE 7 | GATEWAY TO THE DIVINE COLLECTIVE

Here we invite you to awaken to the knowledge that ALL ARE ONE. There is a collective ... no separation. Do you believe the words you speak are just words? Or do you understand the power they hold? You are a powerful Creator. Once you breathe life into your words by speaking them aloud you have set a powerful invocation. You have released the energetic signature of those words into the Universe. And the energy will build as it gathers more energy that is in vibrational coherence with its energetic signatures. Child, by the words you speak you can create peace, love, kindness and happiness in the collective or you can create war, destruction, disease and divisiveness. What you create affects the whole of humanity. Now that you hold this understanding create only from your Divine SoulHeart.

MARCH ANGEL MANTRA

- ❦ *"I am part of the Divine Collective. I choose words and actions that bring love, peace and kindness into the world."*

THIS MONTH'S ANGEL MANTRA ATTUNEMENT

Each morning, look into a mirror, begin taking long, slow, deep breaths all the way into your belly. As you breathe bring your awareness into your SoulHeart. Feel your beautiful SoulHeart expanding. Feel the shift. Do you feel warm ... or cool? Do you feel vibration? See color? Now, bring your awareness back to your breath and take 3 long, slow, deep breaths. On each outbreath, repeat or tone the Angel Mantra out loud:

- ❦ *"I am part of the Divine Collective. I choose words and actions that bring love, peace and kindness into the world."*

Repeat for a total of 3 breaths. For an even deeper alignment, repeat this in the evenings, too!

march

SUNDAY	MONDAY	TUESDAY
1	2	3
8	9 FULL MOON (VIRGO) ANGEL CODES: 7/10 *MERCURY DIRECT*	10
15	16	17
22	23	24 NEW MOON (ARIES) ANGEL CODES: 4/4
29	30	31

2020

WEDNESDAY	THURSDAY	FRIDAY	SATURDAY
4	5	6	7
11	12	13	14
18	19 EQUINOX	20	21
25	26	27	28

MAR

march

S	M	T	W	T	F	S
1	2	3	4	5	6	7
8	9	10	11	12	13	14
15	16	17	18	19	20	21
22	23	24	25	26	27	28
29	30	31				

notes

2 MONDAY	**3** TUESDAY	**4** WEDNESDAY

5 THURSDAY	6 FRIDAY	7 SATURDAY	8 SUNDAY

March Full Moon (Supermoon)

DATE: MONDAY, MARCH 9 / LUNATION: 10:48 AM NEW YORK.
ASTRO SIGN: 19° VIRGO / RULER: MERCURY
ELEMENT: EARTH / EXPRESSION: MUTABLE
ARCHANGEL: MICHAEL

FULL MOON KEYWORDS: COMPLETION, SURRENDER

LUNA'S ASTRO ENERGIES

When Lady Luna is in her Mercury ruled Virgo energies, you may find yourself working so hard, methodically organizing, analyzing everything, and paying great attention to detail that you have forgotten to come up for air. Lady Luna is reminding you to take a deep breath, take time out and play with others!

MARCH 9 VIRGO FULL MOON ANGEL CODE 7/10

OVERLIGHTING ANGEL CODE 7 | GATEWAY TO THE DIVINE COLLECTIVE
Activation: Activates your connection to the Collective Consciousness.

This powerful supermoon Full Moon activates the Overlighting Angel Code of 7, the energetic signature of the Collective Consciousness! Here, you are reminded that you are a being of Divine Energy. You are part of the Divine Collective. Your thoughts and actions are energy forms that affect the whole of life… even the weather!

ARCHANGEL ARIEL'S MESSAGE 7 | GATEWAY OF THE DIVINE COLLECTIVE

Dear One, we invite you to awaken to the knowledge that All Are One. There is a collective … no separation. You are part of the Whole. What you do, what you say and what you think affects the Whole of Life… not just beings who breathe but the mountains, seas, waters, weather. All are a reflection of the energetic signature sent forth. Do you believe the words you speak are just words? Or do you understand the power they hold? You are a powerful creator! Once you breathe life into your words by speaking them aloud you have set a powerful invocation. You have released the energetic signature of those words into the universe. And the energy will build as it gathers more energy that is in vibrational coherence with its energetic signatures. Dear One, by the words you speak you can create Peace, Love, Kindness and Happiness in the collective or you can create

War, Destruction, Disease and Divisiveness. What you create affects the whole of humanity. Keep your thoughts uplifted. Treat others with respect. Care for your planet. Understand All Are One and YOU affect the Whole! Now that you hold this understanding, we know you will create from your Divine SoulHeart.

LUNATION ANGEL CODE 10 | GATEWAY OF THE UNIVERSAL LIGHT STAR
Activation: Activates Light unifying your physical Body Temple with your Light Body, Divine Light of the Universe and all Benevolent Light Beings.

Monday's Full Moon at 19° Virgo activates the ANGEL CODE 10 | UNIVERSAL LIGHT STAR. This is a powerful code transmitting your connection to Universal Light including All Light Beings throughout the Cosmos! And this SUPERMOON is amped even more because both Sun and Moon are activating 10!

ARCHANGEL ARIEL'S MESSAGE 10 | GATEWAY OF THE UNIVERSAL LIGHT STAR

Dear One, Angel Code 10 brings light from the universe into your physical body. Light holds the divine spark … light is energy. Energy of the universe is pouring through your physical Body Temple bringing spirit into matter … illuminating you.

MARCH 9 VIRGO FULL MOON ACTIVATION FOR MATERIAL WEALTH

Full Moons activate completion and surrendering things in your life that no longer serve you. And, Sweet One, always surrendering with love and gratitude. This Full Moon you have the powerful support of Archangel Michael and Lady Luna in her Virgo energies. This Supermoon is the first time this year you are invited to surrender blocks to MATERIAL WEALTH!

Please take some quiet time this week feeling into the **Angel Codes 7 | Gateway to The Divine Collective** and **10 | Gateway of The Universal Light Star.** Feel into **Lady Luna's Astro Energies of Mercury ruled Virgo**. Here Luna is in her earthy energies… very organized, analytical and methodical! How can you use these energies to help you surrender blocks to MATERIAL WEALTH?

Darling Heart, we invite you to spend some quiet time on Monday tuning into your beautiful Infinite Heart, feeling into your dreams and wishes. Feeling into your Material Wealth. On this Full Moon decide on one thing you want to surrender that you believe is keeping you from enjoying an abundance of Materiel Wealth. To help you sort it out, call on Archangel Michael, Angel of Virgo, Angel of Strength and Courage. Here's our checklist:

Material Wealth
On a scale of 1 – 10 what's your number? _____

(10 feeling absolutely Divinely Wealthy, 1 wondering how you are going to pay your bills.)

Darling Heart come to stillness and feel into your relationship with Money. Here are some common thoughts associated with money. Check those that apply:

How I Feel About My Money
I love having enough money to do all the things I love without ever having to think about how much it cost. _____
I just don't have enough for lot of extras. ____
I get a knot in my belly/heart rate shifts when I think about money. _____

Savings
I pay my savings account first. _____
I put money in my savings account every week/paycheck/month. _____
I have a retirement plan. ____
I don't have a solid plan. __
I live from paycheck to paycheck. ____

Purchases
I love new clothes and buy cute things when I see them. _____
I can afford the things I want (gym/classes/conferences/vacations/travel). _____
I rarely buy anything new. _____

Credit Cards
I use my charge accounts and pay them off every month. _____
I use my charge accounts and carry a balance. _____
I use my charge cards and pay the minimum each month. ____

Look at what you've written and name one thing you are willing to surrender this Full Moon that you believe blocks your MATERIAL WEALTH.

_____
_____

MARCH 9 VIRGO FULL MOON FIRE CEREMONY OF SURRENDER

Gather Your Sacred Tools:

❦ The Angel Code Oracle 2020
❦ A candle and lighter

- A fireproof bowl
- A small piece of paper for burning
- A pen or pencil

Darling Heart, go to a space where you won't be disturbed and light your candle. Call in Archangel Michael to help you come fully into your shining heart as you release with love and gratitude. Write whatever you are surrendering on a small slip of paper. Read what you've written out loud. You might use these words:

"By the light of this full moon I surrender _____to the Sacred Fires. I surrender with Love and Gratitude and I am now complete with _____."

Then light your paper and watch it burn. Knowing you have surrendered, released and are now complete. Sit for a moment. Feel into the power of surrender. And now write whatever impressions, feelings and awareness you have.

_____

_____

_____

_____

Thank Archangel Michael and Lady Luna and extinguish your fire.

What to do with the ashes? Many people choose to bury them. I like to go outside by the light of the moon, hold the ashes in my palm and blow them away!

Darling Heart, a surrendering ceremony is really powerful…trust that whatever you have released no longer has power over you and be sure not to re-invoke it into your life!

MAR

march

S	M	T	W	T	F	S
1	2	3	4	5	6	7
8	9	10	11	12	13	14
15	16	17	18	19	20	21
22	23	24	25	26	27	28
29	30	31				

notes

9 MONDAY	**10** TUESDAY	**11** WEDNESDAY
FULL MOON ASTRO SIGN: VIRGO ANGEL CODES: 7/10 *MERCURY DIRECT*		

| 12 | 13 | 14 | 15 |
THURSDAY	FRIDAY	SATURDAY	SUNDAY

MAR
march

S	M	T	W	T	F	S
1	2	3	4	5	6	7
8	9	10	11	12	13	14
15	16	17	18	19	20	21
22	23	24	25	26	27	28
29	30	31				

notes

16 MONDAY	17 TUESDAY	18 WEDNESDAY

19 THURSDAY	**20** FRIDAY	**21** SATURDAY	**22** SUNDAY
EQUINOX			

March New Moon

DATE: TUESDAY, MARCH 24 / LUNATION: 2:29 AM NEW YORK
ASTRO SIGN: 4° ARIES / RULER: MARS
ELEMENT: FIRE / EXPRESSION: CARDINAL
ARCHANGEL: URIEL

NEW MOON KEYWORDS: NEW BEGINNING, CREATION

LUNA'S ASTRO ENERGIES

Our first New Moon in this new season! Spring has arrived! Lady Luna is shining her light through Mars ruled Aries stirring your passion and up-leveling your confidence. You may feel especially courageous, motivated by wild enthusiasm, you just can't wait to begin that new project, relationship, or just something new!

MARCH 24 ARIES NEW MOON ANGEL CODE 4/4

Oh My! Another powerful amplification of Codes!!! BOTH the Overlighting Angel Code and the Lunation Angel Code are 4 | GATEWAY TO THE INFINITE HEART. And, of course, the Sun is also activating this 4!

OVERLIGHTING and LUNATION ANGEL CODE 4 | GATEWAY TO THE INFINITE HEART
Activation: Activating your Light of Infinite Love shining through your Infinite SoulHeart.

Tuesday's New Moon at 4° Aries activates the ANGEL CODE 4 | Gateway To The Infinite Heart. The energetic signature of this code is amplified FOUR times! Moon at 4° Aries, Sun at 4° Aries, the overlighting code for this lunation is 4 AND the 2020 ANGEL CODE is 4! Sound familiar? We experienced these same energetic signatures last month during the New Moon in Pisces lunation. Each time we experience repeating energetic signatures we are offered an opportunity to go even deeper in our understanding!

ARCHANGEL ARIEL'S MESSAGE 4 | GATEWAY TO THE INFINITE HEART

Dear One, in the timing of this New Moon there is much amplification of your Infinite Heart carrying forth from the February 23rd New Moon in the last lunar cycle. Here it comes forth merging with the energies of Infinite Possibilities. Remember Dear One, you are an infinite being created out of the Divine …. You are limitless … You are Infinite Heart aligning with Infinite Possibilities! This is how you arrived on your beautiful blue planet. Do not place limits upon yourself. This is a planet of free will. Surrender ties you have used to bind your creativity …. And create now the passions of your soul… Your dreams …. Your wishes. You are a powerful Infinite Creator!

MARCH 24 ARIES NEW MOON ACTIVATION FOR MATERIAL WEALTH

New Moon activates new beginnings, visioning, setting goals and creating while you have the powerful support of Archangel Uriel and Lady Luna. On the last Full Moon, you were invited to surrender something that blocks your MATERIAL WEALTH so now, on this New Moon, we invite you to create more wealth in your life!

As we move through the Wheel of the Year, this New Moon is the first time we are inviting you to create more MATERIAL WEALTH!

Please take some quiet time this week feeling into the **Angel Code 4 | Gateway To The Infinite Heart**. Feel into the **Lady Luna's Astro Energies of Mars ruled Aries**. Here Luna is in on Fire and ready to ignite your dreams! How can these energies help you create more MATERIAL WEALTH?

Darling Heart, we invite you to spend some quiet time on Tuesday tuning into your beautiful Infinite Heart, feeling into your dreams and wishes around your Wealth. Call on Archangel Uriel, Angel of Aries, Angel of Light and Clarity to help you clarify the change you are making as you create more MATERIAL WEALTH!

Sweet One, ask yourself the following questions:

Material Wealth
On a scale of 1 – 10 what's your number? _____
(10 feeling absolutely divinely wealthy, 1 wondering how you are going to pay your bills)

And now, come to stillness and feel into your relationship with Money. Here are some common thoughts associated with money. Check those that apply:

How I Feel About My Money
I love having enough money to do all the things I love without ever having to think about
    how much it cost. _____
I just don't have enough for lots of extras. ____
I get a knot in my belly / heart rate shifts when I think about money. __

Savings

I pay my savings account first. _____

I put money in my savings account every week/paycheck/month. _____

I have a retirement plan. ____

I don't have a solid plan. __

I live from paycheck to paycheck. ____

Purchases

I love new clothes and buy cute things when I see them. _____

I can afford the things I want (gym/classes/conferences/vacations/travel). __

I rarely buy anything new. __

Credit Cards

I use my charge accounts and pay them off every month. _____

I use my charge accounts and carry a balance. _____

I use my charge cards and pay the minimum each month. ___

From the questions above write down 3 possible areas where you can create even more MATERIAL WEALTH.

_____

_____

_____

Read each possibility out loud. Feel into them. Does one stand out from the other two? Does one bring a smile as you read it? Is one easier to manifest? Or do you feel the timing is right... Or not?

Which possibility on your list of 3 is the one to activate during this lunar cycle?

_____

_____

MARCH 24 ARIES NEW MOON CEREMONY OF CREATION

Gather Your Sacred Tools:

- The Angel Code Oracle 2020
- A candle and lighter
- Paper, pens, markers etc.
- A pen or pencil

Sweet One, go to a space where you won't be disturbed and light your candle. Call in Archangel Uriel to help inspire you as you come fully into your shining heart preparing to activate your New Moon dream! Allow yourself plenty of time to play with this!

Review the possibility you decided to activate during this lunar cycle and write a creation statement (an intention) to activate more MATERIAL WEALTH. Remember your statement is to be in the present and not in the future!

_____

OK, Dear Heart, now let's turn that intention into a goal with 3 actionable steps!

3 Actions I Am Taking in the next two weeks to manifest more MATERIAL WEALTH!

_____

_____

_____

Awesome! You now have a goal and 3 actionable steps to take!

Here's the next part of your New Moon Creation Ceremony! We invite you to create a mini angel board! It's a vision board with the Angels! On your paper using your pens and markers write your intention and the 3 actions you are taking in the next two weeks!

Be sure to write Thank You on your board. You can write a simple Thank You or something more elaborate, "Thank You Angels and Lady Luna for this and all deliciousness I'm creating now!"

Be creative! Create something you'd like to look at least once a day, each and EVERY day! Make it fun … catchy … playful!!

When you've completed your mini angel board put your tools away.

Thank Archangel Uriel and Lady Luna and extinguish your candle.

Be sure to place your Angel Board where you will see it every day for the next two weeks!

Here are some things you might like to do to keep your mini angel board in your awareness:

- ❧ Take a picture on your phone and make it your screen saver.
- ❧ Take a photo on your computer and make it your screen saver.

- ❦ Frame it and put it on your desk or in your kitchen.
- ❦ Keep it on your bed stand. It's great seeing it first thing in the morning and again, just before falling asleep!

Dear Heart, FOLLOW YOUR ACTIONABLE STEPS! When you DO something toward your goals you are actually creating an energetic alignment. And you know alignment helps you manifest more quickly!

Our FREE Thank You Gift for You!

We've created 2 amazing video gifts to help you make 2020 an absolutely deliciously magical year! To receive your FREE videos, please e-mail us at the e-mail address below and we'll send your free videos directly to your inbox!

- ❦ How-To Use Angel Code Oracle 2020
      To receive this video please send your e-mail to:
      Taco2020How-To@katebeloved.com
- ❦ 3-Video Angel Code Masterclass
      To receive this video please send your e-mail to:
      Taco2020MasterClass@katebeloved.com

Wishing you an absolutely delicious 2020!

Abundant Angel Blessings
Beloved

MAR
march

S	M	T	W	T	F	S
1	2	3	4	5	6	7
8	9	10	11	12	13	14
15	16	17	18	19	20	21
22	23	24	25	26	27	28
29	30	31				

notes

23 MONDAY	**24** TUESDAY	**25** WEDNESDAY
	NEW MOON	
	ASTRO SIGN: ARIES	
	ANGEL CODES: 4/4	

26 THURSDAY	**27** FRIDAY	**28** SATURDAY	**29** SUNDAY

April 2020 Overlighting Angel Code
8 | Gateway of Infinite Possibilities

Activation: Activates your limitless possibilities. Life on Earth is meant to be lived with infinite abundance!

Our Overlighting Angel Code for the month of April 2020 is 8 | GATEWAY OF INFINITE POSSIBILITIES. This month you are invited to connect to your Infinite Soul, replenishing yourself as the Light of Infinite Possibilities flows through your entire system. When this light flows free you can access your Soul Experiences.

ARCHANGEL ARIEL'S MESSAGE 8 | GATEWAY OF INFINITE POSSIBILITIES

You, Dear One, are a Divine Being holding the Light of Infinite Possibilities. When you chose to incarnate on planet Earth you chose to experience all delights this magical blue planet has to offer… creating an abundant, joyful, vibrantly healthy, loving life for yourself! As a Cosmic Soul you were aware only of limitless infinite possibility. This month we invite you to return to the knowing that there are no limits and your life Is truly filled with infinite possibilities awaiting you to choose the ones to activate!

APRIL ANGEL MANTRA

- *"I am an Infinite Being with no beginning and no end. My life is filled with Infinite Possibilities."*

THIS MONTH'S ANGEL MANTRA ACTIVATION

Each morning this month, look into a mirror, begin taking long, slow, deep breaths all the way into your belly. As you breathe bring your awareness into your SoulHeart. Feel your beautiful Soul-Heart expanding. Feel the shift. Do you feel warm … Or cool? Do you feel vibration? See color? Now, bring your awareness back to your breath and take 3 long, slow, deep breaths. On each outbreath, repeat or tone the Angel Mantra out loud:

- *"I am an Infinite Being with no beginning and no end. My life is filled with Infinite Possibilities."*

Repeat for a total of 3 breaths. For an even deeper alignment, repeat this in the evenings, too!

april

This Month

_____

_____

_____

_____

_____

_____

_____

_____

_____

_____

_____

_____

SUNDAY	MONDAY	TUESDAY
5	6	7 FULL MOON (LIBRA) ANGEL CODES: 6/9
12	13	14
19	20	21
26	27	28

2020

WEDNESDAY	THURSDAY	FRIDAY	SATURDAY
1	2	3	4
8	9	10	11
15	16	17	18
22 NEW MOON (TAURUS) ANGEL CODES: 12/3	23	24	25
29	30		

APR

april

S	M	T	W	T	F	S
			1	2	3	4
5	6	7	8	9	10	11
12	13	14	15	16	17	18
19	20	21	22	23	24	25
26	27	28	29	30		

notes

30 MONDAY	**31** TUESDAY	**1** WEDNESDAY

2 THURSDAY	**3** FRIDAY	**4** SATURDAY	**5** SUNDAY

April Full Moon (Supermoon)

DATE: TUESDAY, APRIL 7 / LUNATION: 7:36 PM NEW YORK
ASTRO SIGN: 18° LIBRA / RULER: VENUS
ELEMENT: AIR / EXPRESSION: CARDINAL
ARCHANGEL: GABRIEL

FULL MOON KEYWORDS: COMPLETION, SURRENDER

LUNA'S ASTRO ENERGIES

Darling Heart, on this full moon lunation Lady Luna is inviting you to take a feel into Libra energies. When Lady Luna is flowing through Libra, she is cooperative, gracious, balanced and the queen of the ball! During this lunation, she is reminding you to avoid conflict and to surrender anything that keeps you from your peace.

APRIL 7 LIBRA FULL MOON ANGEL CODE 6/9

OVERLIGHTING ANGEL CODE 6 | GATEWAY OF INFINITE KNOWING
Activation: Activates your intuition in all realms and dimensions.

Darling Heart Spirit! You came to earth to experience a life on the material plane, yet you are a very powerful intuitive! Intuitive knowing is one of your many gifts of spirit! This month, you're invited to reawaken your infinite knowing. The angels are reminding you that you are a magnificent Spirit Being experiencing a life in matter. You are one with the Universe and all can be known. Remember, Dear Heart, you are a Master Intuitive.

ARCHANGEL ARIEL'S MESSAGE 6 | GATEWAY OF INFINITE KNOWING

Dear One, remember you are a masterful intuitive being. You are not of the earth. Yet part of you is in your earth body … There is so much more. You are a masterful intuitive and as you awaken, you will tune into the infinite knowing … unexpected at first and then proceeding at will. Opening your God's Eye of Infinite Knowing connects you to the Whole of Life and the Whole of Your Being!

LUNATION ANGEL CODE 9 | GATEWAY OF DIVINE BLESSINGS
Activation: Activates your soul gifts and communication with benevolent Cosmic Beings; Angels, Star Beings, and Unseen Guides.

Sweet One, you are receiving blessings from the Divine! These blessings are an opportunity for you to awaken your soul gifts including communicating with all the angels, star beings and guides throughout the Cosmos. And, Darling Heart, energies are AMPLIFIED!... This is our second consecutive SUPERMOON!! And this Code is amplified because both the Sun and Moon are activating the 9!

ARCHANGEL ARIEL'S MESSAGE 9 | GATEWAY OF DIVINE BLESSINGS

Dear One, you are a Divine Being of Spirit. You have many SOUL gifts; some are known to you and some are not. You have the ability to connect with all angels, star beings and guides throughout the cosmos. These benevolent beings are here awaiting your invitation to join you on your Earth journey.

APRIL 7 LIBRA FULL MOON ACTIVATION FOR LOVE

Full Moons activate completion and surrendering things in your life that no longer serve a purpose. And, of course, Sweet One, always surrender with love and gratitude. You now have the powerful support of Archangel Gabriel and Lady Luna in her Libra energies. This Full Moon you are invited for the second time this year to surrender blocks to Love!

Please take some quiet time this week feeling into the **Angel Codes 6 | Gateway Of Infinite Knowing** and **9 | Gateway Of Divine Blessings**. Feel into **Lady Luna's Astro Energies of Venus ruled Libra**. Here Luna flies through the air socializing with all she sees out in the Cosmos. She creates through communication. She creates balance, beauty and love. Her quicksilver mind comes up with all sorts of creative ideas! How can you use these energies to help you surrender blocks to LOVE?

Darling Heart, we invite you to spend some quiet time on Tuesday tuning into your beautiful Infinite Heart, feeling into your dreams and wishes. Feeling into Love. On this Full Moon, decide on one thing you want to surrender that you believe is keeping your Heart from experiencing its most delicious Love and Joy. To help you sort it out, call on Archangel Gabriel, angel of Libra, angel of divine messages and inspiration. For this Full Moon, your second opportunity this year to surrender blocks to Love, let's focus on how you express Love! Here's are some things to consider:

What is your passion? _____

_____

What makes your heart sing? _____

_____

What are your favorite ways of expressing romantic love?

    writing__ art__ music__ talking__ singing__ dancing__ touching__ eye-gazing__ sex__

    other_____

What are your favorite ways of expressing non-romantic love?

    writing__ art__ music__ talking__ singing__ dancing__ touching__ eye-gazing__

    other _____

BONUS QUESTION

On a scale of 1-10 How much do you love yourself? What's your number? _____

(10 is *Yes! I'm absolutely, totally awesome!* 1 is *I'm a mess. Totally unworthy of love.*)

If you rated yourself less than 10, what is keeping you from absolutely adoring your totally awesome self?

_____

_____

Look at what you've written and create one thing you are willing to surrender that you believe blocks LOVE in your life.

_____

APRIL 7 LIBRA FULL MOON FIRE CEREMONY OF SURRENDER

Gather Your Sacred Tools:

- The Angel Code Oracle 2020
- A candle and lighter
- A fireproof bowl
- A small piece of paper for burning
- A pen or pencil

Go to a space where you won't be disturbed and light your candle. Call in Archangel Gabriel to help you come fully into your shining heart as you release with love and gratitude. Write whatever you are surrendering on a small slip of paper. Read what you've written out loud. You might use these words:

"By the light of this full moon I surrender _____to the Sacred Fires. I surrender with Love and Gratitude and I am now complete with _____."

Then light your paper and watch it burn. Knowing you have surrendered, released and are now complete. Sit for a moment. Feel into the power of surrender. And now write whatever impressions, feelings and awareness you have. _____

_____

Thank Archangel Gabriel and Lady Luna and extinguish your fire.

What to do with the ashes? Many people choose to bury them. I like to go outside by the light of the moon, hold the ashes in my palm and blow them away!

Darling Heart, a surrendering ceremony is really powerful…trust that whatever you have released no longer has power over you and be sure not to re-invoke it into your life!

APR

april

S	M	T	W	T	F	S
		1	2	3	4	
5	6	7	8	9	10	11
12	13	14	15	16	17	18
19	20	21	22	23	24	25
26	27	28	29	30		

notes

6
MONDAY

7
TUESDAY

FULL MOON

ASTRO SIGN: LIBRA

ANGEL CODES: 6/9

8
WEDNESDAY

9	10	11	12
THURSDAY	FRIDAY	SATURDAY	SUNDAY

APR

april

S	M	T	W	T	F	S
		1	2	3	4
5	6	7	8	9	10	11
12	13	14	15	16	17	18
19	20	21	22	23	24	25
26	27	28	29	30		

notes

13 MONDAY	14 TUESDAY	15 WEDNESDAY

16 THURSDAY	**17** FRIDAY	**18** SATURDAY	**19** SUNDAY

April New Moon

DATE: WEDNESDAY, APRIL 22 / LUNATION: 7:27 PM NEW YORK
ASTRO SIGN: 3° TAURUS / RULER: VENUS
ELEMENT: EARTH / EXPRESSION: FIXED
ARCHANGEL: MICHAEL

NEW MOON KEY WORDS: NEW BEGINNING, CREATION

LUNA'S ASTRO ENERGIES

When Lady Luna is in Venus ruled Taurus, she loves to be surrounded by love, luxury, beauty and material delights! During this new moon, Lady Luna invites you to look at your surroundings, your environment and your home. How can you beautify them? How could you bring a bit of luxury into your environment? Remember Darling Heart, only bring in things you love!

APRIL 22 TAURUS NEW MOON ANGEL CODE 12/3

OVERLIGHTING ANGEL CODE 12 | GATEWAY TO THE HEART OF THE DIVINE MOTHER
Activation: Activates direct connection to the Divine through the Divine Mother Essence.

During this New Moon, Luna is activating direct connection to the Divine through the essence of the Divine Mother.

ARCHANGEL ARIEL'S MESSAGE 12 | GATEWAY TO THE HEART OF THE DIVINE MOTHER

Here we have the energetic signature of the Divine Mother… the essence of divinity of The All… of God, Goddess, Creator, Source, however you understand THE ONE. Understand this energy not as a mother you have known in physical form, but as a Divine Mother who comes in with the energetic signature of the Divine Creator and invites you to open to the qualities of the Divine Feminine … to understand that your world must now live through the SoulHeart. To live the qualities of the empowered mother… of divine feminine …. Those qualities of unconditional love … of honoring … cooperation … respect … and allowing others to be what they are meant to be … to live their lives following their own paths … and to live your earth journey in your way … knowing that you are a multidimensional Divine Spiritual Being. Through the frequencies of the Divine Mother essence you are also connected to all essences of the divine … you are one with Divine Energy.

LUNATION ANGEL CODE 3 | GATEWAY OF THE ILLUMINATED SELF
Activation: Activates Self-Empowerment as your embodied Light merges with the Divine All.

Wednesday's New Moon ACTIVATES the energetic signature of Angel Code 3, the Angel Code empowering self as your embodied light merges with the Divine All and connects you to The All. And, of course, this is amped up because both Sun and Moon are activating the 3!

ARCHANGEL ARIEL'S MESSAGE 3 | GATEWAY OF THE ILLUMINATED SELF

Dear One, this code merges your Illuminated Self with the Divine Mother. Here you are brought into direct connection to the divine through the Divine Mother essence. As you feel into these frequencies, understand you are not alone. You came to earth with a whole team guiding you. Not only angels, the ascended masters are here too. So, we invite you to call on the masters. There are many. Who resonates with you? Quan Yin? Yogananda? Yeshua/Jesus? Mary? There are many. You have lived many lifetimes and have related with your guides through eons. And Dear One, there is no right or wrong. Call on those connected to your SoulHeart.

APRIL 22 TAURUS NEW MOON ACTIVATION FOR LOVE

New Moon activates new beginnings, visioning, setting goals and creating while you have the powerful support of Archangel Michael and Lady Luna. As we move through the Wheel of the Year, this New Moon is your second opportunity to focus on manifesting more LOVE in your life!

Please take some quiet time this week feeling into the **Angel Codes 12 | Gateway To The Heart of the Divine Mother** and **3 | Gateway To The Illuminated Self**. Feel into **Lady Luna's Astro Energies of Venus ruled Taurus**. When Luna is in her Earthy Taurus energies, she loves maintaining herself in Love and Beauty! How can these energies help you activate more LOVE?

Darling Heart, we invite you to spend some quiet time on Wednesday tuning into your beautiful Infinite Heart, feeling into your dreams and wishes. Feeling in to LOVE. Call on Archangel Michael, Angel of Taurus, Angel of Strength and Courage to bring you strength and courage to call in your dreams!

And now, Sweet One, ask yourself the following questions:

What is your passion? _____

_____

What makes your heart sing? _____

_____

What makes you feel loved? _____
_____

What makes you feel beautiful? _____
_____

How can you bring more of that into your life during this Lunar cycle? _____
_____

From the above questions write down 3 dreams you'd like to create to bring more LOVE into your life!
_____
_____
_____

Read each dream out loud. Feel into them. Does one stand out from the other two? Does one bring a smile as you read it? Is one easier to manifest? Or do you feel the timing is right… Or not?

Which dream on your list of 3 is the one to activate during this lunar cycle?
_____

APRIL 22 TAURUS NEW MOON CEREMONY OF CREATION

Gather Your Sacred Tools:

- The Angel Code Oracle 2020
- A candle and lighter
- Paper, pens, markers etc.
- A pen or pencil

Sweet One, go to a space where you won't be disturbed and light your candle. Call in Archangel Michael to help inspire you as you come fully into your shining heart preparing to activate your New Moon dream! Allow yourself plenty of time to play with this!

Review the dream you decided to activate during this lunar cycle and write a creation statement (an intention) to create more LOVE into your life. Remember your statement is to be in the present and not in the future!

_____
_____

OK, Dear Heart, now let's turn that intention into a goal with 3 actionable steps!

3 actions I am taking in the next two weeks to manifest my intention to bring more delicious LOVE in my life!

_____

_____

_____

Awesome! You now have a goal and 3 actionable steps to take!

Here's the next part of your New Moon Creation Ceremony! We invite you to create a mini angel board! It's a vision board with the Angels! On your paper using your pens and markers write your intention and the 3 actions you are taking in the next two weeks!

Be sure to write Thank You on your board. You can write a simple Thank You or something more elaborate, "Thank You Angels and Lady Luna for this and all deliciousness I'm creating now!"

Be creative! Create something you'd like to look at least once a day, each and EVERY day! Make it fun … catchy … playful!!

When you've completed your mini angel board put your tools away.

Thank Archangel Michael and Lady Luna and extinguish your candle.

Be sure to place your Angel Board where you will see it every day for the next two weeks!
Here are some things you might like to do to keep your mini angel board in your awareness:

- Take a picture on your phone and make it your screen saver.
- Take a photo on your computer and make it your screen saver.
- Frame it and put it on your desk or in your kitchen.
- Keep it on your bed stand. It's great seeing it first thing in the morning and again just before falling asleep!

Dear Heart, FOLLOW YOUR ACTIONABLE STEPS! When you DO something toward your goals you are actually creating an energetic alignment. And you know alignment helps you manifest more quickly!

APR

april

S	M	T	W	T	F	S
		1	2	3	4	
5	6	7	8	9	10	11
12	13	14	15	16	17	18
19	20	21	22	23	24	25
26	27	28	29	30		

notes

20 MONDAY

21 TUESDAY

22 WEDNESDAY

NEW MOON

ASTRO SIGN: TAURUS

ANGEL CODES: 12/3

23 THURSDAY	**24** FRIDAY	**25** SATURDAY	**26** SUNDAY

APR

april

S	M	T	W	T	F	S
			1	2	3	4
5	6	7	8	9	10	11
12	13	14	15	16	17	18
19	20	21	22	23	24	25
26	27	28	29	30		

notes

27 MONDAY	28 TUESDAY	29 WEDNESDAY

30 THURSDAY	**1** FRIDAY	**2** SATURDAY	**3** SUNDAY

May 2020 Overlighting Angel Code
9 | Gateway of Divine Blessings

Activation: Activates your soul gifts and communication with benevolent Cosmic Beings; Angels, Star Beings and Unseen Guides.

Darling Heart, this month's Overlighting Angel Code 9 activates Blessings of the Divine as they pour forth for you. These blessings are an opportunity for you to awaken your soul gifts including communicating with all the angels, star beings and guides throughout the Cosmos.

ARCHANGEL ARIEL'S MESSAGE 9 | GATEWAY OF DIVINE BLESSINGS

Remember, Dear One, you are not a Being of Matter you are a Being of Spirit with many soul gifts. When you return to your soul understanding and access this Soul Star Portal you can choose to be in communication with beings throughout the Galaxies … ALL Angels, Star Beings and Guides.

MAY ANGEL MANTRA

🦋 *"As I practice my daily attunements my Earth Being merges with my Spirit and I have easy access to my Soul Gifts!"*

THIS MONTH'S ANGEL MANTRA ACTIVATION

Each morning this month, look into a mirror, begin taking long, slow, deep breaths all the way into your belly. As you breathe bring your awareness into your SoulHeart. Feel your beautiful Soul-Heart expanding. Feel the shift. Do you feel warm… or cool? Do you feel vibration? See color? Now, bring your awareness back to your breath and take 3 long, slow, deep breaths. On each outbreath, repeat or tone the Angel Mantra out loud:

🦋 *"As I practice my daily attunements my Earth Being merges with my Spirit and I have easy access to my Soul Gifts!"*

Repeat for a total of 3 breaths. For an even deeper alignment, repeat this in the evenings, too!

may

This Month

SUNDAY	MONDAY	TUESDAY
3	4	5
10	11	12
17	18	19
24	25	26
31		

2020

WEDNESDAY	THURSDAY	FRIDAY	SATURDAY
		1	2
6	7 FULL MOON (SCORPIO) ANGEL CODES: 7/8	8	9
13	14	15	16
20	21	22 NEW MOON (GEMINI) ANGEL CODES: 4/2	23
27	28	29	30

May Full Moon

DATE: THURSDAY, MAY 7 / LUNATION: 3:45 AM (NEW YORK)
ASTRO SIGN: 17° SCORPIO / RULER: MARS / PLUTO
ELEMENT: WATER / EXPRESSION: FIXED
ARCHANGEL: RAPHAEL

FULL MOON KEYWORDS: COMPLETION, SURRENDER

LUNA'S ASTRO ENERGIES

Lady Luna is activating Pluto/Mars ruled Scorpio. Passions run hot. At this Lunar Portal of surrender you are being invited to surrender what is complete. Lady Luna in Watery Scorpio shines her light on your deep emotions. Is there something that brings fear? Do you feel indecisive? Is there some place in your life where you are not authentic? Accept Lady Luna's invitation to explore these areas.

MAY 7 SCORPIO FULL MOON ANGEL CODE 7/8

OVERLIGHTING ANGEL CODE 7 | GATEWAY TO THE DIVINE COLLECTIVE
Activation: Activates your connection to the Collective Consciousness.

This Full Moon activates the Overlighting Angel Code of 7, the energetic signature of the Collective Consciousness! Here, you are reminded that you are a being of Divine Energy. You are part of the Divine Collective. Your thoughts and actions are energy forms that affect the whole of life … even the weather!

ARCHANGEL ARIEL'S MESSAGE 7 | GATEWAY TO THE DIVINE COLLECTIVE

Dear One, we invite you to awaken to the knowledge that all are one. There is a collective … no separation. Do you believe the words you speak are just words? Or do you understand the power they hold? You are a powerful creator! Once you breathe life into your words by speaking them aloud you have set a powerful invocation. You have released the energetic signature of those words into the universe. And the energy will build as it gathers more energy that is in vibrational coherence with its energetic signatures. Dear one, by the words you speak you can create Peace, Love, Kindness and Happiness in the collective or you can create war, destruction, disease and divisiveness. What you create affects the whole of humanity. Now that you hold this understanding, we know you will create from your divine SoulHeart.

LUNATION ANGEL CODE 8 | GATEWAY OF INFINITE POSSIBILITIES
Activation: Activates your limitless possibilities. Life on Earth is meant to be lived with infinite abundance!

During this full moon you are invited to connect to your Infinite Soul, replenishing you as the Light of Infinite Possibilities flows through your entire system. When this light flows through you can access your Soul Experiences. And, this code is amplified because both Sun and Moon are activating the 8!

ARCHANGEL ARIEL'S MESSAGE 8 | GATEWAY OF INFINITE POSSIBILITIES

You, Dear One are a Divine Being holding the light of infinite possibilities. When you chose to incarnate on planet Earth you chose to experience all the delights this magical blue planet has to offer … creating an abundant, joyful, vibrantly healthy, loving life for yourself! As a cosmic soul you were aware only of limitless, infinite possibility. We invite you to return to the knowing that there are no limits and your life is truly filled with infinite possibilities awaiting you to choose the ones to activate!

MAY 7 SCORPIO FULL MOON ACTIVATION FOR VIBRANT HEALTH

Full Moons activate completion and surrendering things in your life that no longer serve a purpose. And, of course, Sweet One, always surrender with love and gratitude. You now have the powerful support of Archangel Raphael and Lady Luna in her Scorpio energies. We are inviting you, this Full Moon, for the second time, to surrender habits and choices that block your Vibrant Health! And, of course, Sweet One, Vibrant Health is more than physical well-being! It's your whole self… mind… body… and soul!

Please take some quiet time this week feeling into the **Angel Codes 7 | Gateway To The Divine Collective** and **8 | Gateway Of Infinite Possibilities**. Feel into **Lady Luna's Astro Energies of Pluto/ Mars ruled Scorpio**. Here Luna is in the watery depths of her soul! She is honest and brave. How can you use these energies to help you surrender blocks to your VIBRANT HEALTH?

Darling Heart, we invite you to spend some quiet time on Thursday tuning into your beautiful Infinite Heart, feeling into your dreams and wishes. Feeling into your Health. On this Full Moon decide on one thing you want to surrender that you believe is keeping you from experiencing your perfect Vibrant Health! To help you look deep within, call on Archangel Raphael, Angel of Scorpio, Angel of the Heart, Angel of Love, Healing and Forgiveness. To help you even more here's our checklist:

On a scale of 1 – 10 what's your number? _____
(10 is absolutely perfect vibrant health, 1 is being treated for illness.)

Darling Heart here are some things to consider:

How often are you moving your body? (yoga, tai chi, qigong, running, walking, gym exercise, etc) 1x week___ 3x week_____ more than 3x week___ I'm inconsistent__ not at all ___

Are you eating foods to keep you vibrant? yes___ no__

Are you underweight? ___ overweight? _____

Do you meditate? 1x week___ 3x week___ more than 3x week__ I'm inconsistent__ not at all __

Are you sleeping well? yes ___ no __ sometimes _____

How much time do you spend on your screen/devices daily? minutes __hours__

Are you balancing work and play/family/friends? yes __ no__

Are you leaking energy by holding on to anger, blame, disappointment or loss? _____ yes __ no __

Are you holding on to guilt? ___ yes _____ no

Look at what you've written and name one thing you are willing to surrender this Full Moon that you believe blocks your VIBRANT HEALTH.

_____

_____

MAY 7 SCORPIO FULL MOON FIRE CEREMONY OF SURRENDER

Gather Your Sacred Tools:

- The Angel Code Oracle 2020
- A candle and lighter
- A fireproof bowl
- A small piece of paper for burning
- A pen or pencil

Sweet One, go to a space where you won't be disturbed and light your candle. Call in Archangel Raphael to help you come fully into your shining heart as you release with love and gratitude. Write whatever you are surrendering on a small slip of paper. Read what you've written out loud. You might use these words:

"By the light of this full moon I surrender _____to the Sacred Fires. I surrender with Love and Gratitude and I am now complete with _____."

Then light your paper and watch it burn. Knowing you have surrendered, released and are now complete. Sit for a moment. Feel into the power of surrender. And now write whatever impressions, feelings, and awareness you have.

_____

_____

_____

_____

Thank Archangel Raphael and Lady Luna and extinguish your fire.

What to do with the ashes? Many people choose to bury them. I like to go outside by the light of the moon, hold the ashes in my palm and blow them away!

Darling Heart, a surrendering ceremony is really powerful … trust that whatever you have released no longer has power over you and be sure not to re-invoke it into your life!

MAY

may

S	M	T	W	T	F	S
					1	2
3	4	5	6	7	8	9
10	11	12	13	14	15	16
17	18	19	20	21	22	23
24	25	26	27	28	29	30
31						

notes

4 MONDAY	5 TUESDAY	6 WEDNESDAY

7 THURSDAY	**8** FRIDAY	**9** SATURDAY	**10** SUNDAY
FULL MOON ASTRO SIGN: SCORPIO ANGEL CODES: 7/8			

MAY

may

S	M	T	W	T	F	S
					1	2
3	4	5	6	7	8	9
10	11	12	13	14	15	16
17	18	19	20	21	22	23
24	25	26	27	28	29	30
31						

11
MONDAY

12
TUESDAY

13
WEDNESDAY

notes

14 THURSDAY	**15** FRIDAY	**16** SATURDAY	**17** SUNDAY

May New Moon

DATE: FRIDAY, MAY 22 / LUNATION: 10:39 AM (NEW YORK)
ASTRO SIGN: 2° GEMINI / RULER: MERCURY
ELEMENT: AIR / EXPRESSION: MUTABLE
ARCHANGEL: GABRIEL

NEW MOON KEYWORDS: NEW BEGINNINGS, CREATION

LUNA'S ASTRO ENERGIES

When Lady Luna is bringing forth new beginnings through her Gemini frequencies, she brings you her quick mind and fun-loving wit. Time to create with the support of Lady Luna and these sociable, affectionate and versatile Gemini twins!

MAY 22 GEMINI NEW MOON ANGEL CODE 4/2

OVERLIGHTING ANGEL CODE 4 | GATEWAY TO THE INFINITE HEART
Activation: Activating your Light of Infinite Love shining through your Infinite SoulHeart.

ARCHANGEL ARIEL'S MESSAGE 4 | GATEWAY TO THE INFINITE HEART

Remember, Dear One, you are a Divine Being choosing a life in the physical form. It is your Infinite SoulHeart that is meant to guide you. For you are meant to live on your planet as a Divine Being experiencing the most delicious life you can imagine. Dear One, only a portion of your Divine Being is within your physical form. You have many waiting to serve you … Angels, guides, ascended masters, cosmic beings … Your connection to all of your soul gifts and talents is through your magnificent heart. Let your heart be your guide. When things feel resonant, move forward. When you are feeling discord, retreat. Allow your awareness of your SoulHeart frequency to grow. When you are not sure, feel into your Infinite SoulHeart. Ask questions. Feel into your heart. You will become more skilled as you practice.

LUNATION ANGEL CODE 2 | GATEWAY TO THE SACRED WOMB
Activation: Activates the creation of physical form through the sacred union of Divine Male and Divine Female.

This is an angel code of creation, creating form through the sacred union of divine male and divine female … bringing to life new creations! And, this code is amplified because both sun and moon are activating the 2!

ARCHANGEL ARIEL'S MESSAGE 2 | GATEWAY TO THE SACRED WOMB

Dear One, the energetic signature of this angel code merges Divine Male and Divine Female to bring forth creation! At this New Moon as Luna shines her Light through Gemini, you are invited to come into your Sacred Womb. The place where Divine Male and Divine Female are united. Dear One, you are a Divine Being created from the flame of the Divine, know that you have the power to create without limits! Create your life with passion and joy! What will you create? How will you assist your Sacred Womb in creating your Heart's Desire?

MAY 22 GEMINI NEW MOON ACTIVATION FOR VIBRANT HEALTH

New Moon activates new beginnings, visioning, setting goals and creating while you have the powerful support of Archangel Gabriel and Lady Luna. As we move through the Wheel of the Year, this New Moon is the second time we are inviting you to uplevel your VIBRANT HEALTH! And, of course, Sweet One, VIBRANT HEALTH is more than physical well-being! It's your whole self … mind … body … and soul!

Please take some quiet time this week feeling into the **Angel Codes 4 | Gateway To The Infinite Heart** and **2 | Gateway To The Sacred Womb.** Feel into **Lady Luna's Astro Energies of Mercury ruled Gemini**. Here Luna flies through the Air socializing with all she sees out in the Cosmos. Her quicksilver mind comes up with all sorts of creative ideas! How can these energies help you activate more VIBRANT HEALTH?

Darling Heart, we invite you to spend some quiet time on Friday tuning into your beautiful Infinite Heart, feeling into your dreams and wishes around your Health. Call on Archangel Gabriel, Angel of Gemini, Angel of Divine Inspiration to inspire you as you create more VIBRANT HEALTH!

Sweet One, ask yourself the following questions:

On a scale of 1 – 10 what's your number? _____
(10 is absolutely perfect vibrant health, 1 is being treated for illness)

And now, come to stillness and feel into your relationship with Your Health. Here are some common questions associated with Health. Check those that apply:

How often are you moving your body? (yoga, tai chi, qigong, running, walking, gym exercise, etc.) 1x week____ 3x week____ more than 3x week____ I'm inconsistent__

Not at all _

Are you eating foods to keep you vibrant? yes__no__

Are you underweight? ____ overweight?_____

Do you meditate? 1x week____ 3x week__ more than 3x week__ I'm inconsistent__

not at all __

Are you sleeping well? yes ____ no __ sometimes _____

How much time do you spend on your screen/devices daily? minutes __hours __

Are you balancing work and play/family/friends? yes __ no__

Are you leaking energy by holding on to anger, blame, disappointment or loss? yes__ no __

Are you holding on to guilt? yes __ no__

From the list above write down 3 possibilities where you can create more Vibrant Health.

_____

_____

_____

Read each possibility out loud. Feel into them. Does one stand out from the other two? Does one bring a smile as you read it? Is one easier to manifest? Or do you feel the timing is right… Or not?

Which possibility on your list of 3 is the one to activate during this lunar cycle?

_____

_____

MAY 22 GEMINI NEW MOON CEREMONY OF CREATION

Gather Your Sacred Tools:

- The Angel Code Oracle 2020
- A candle and lighter
- Paper, pens, markers etc.
- A pen or pencil

Sweet One, go to a space where you won't be disturbed and light your candle. Call in Archangel Gabriel to help inspire you as you come fully into your shining heart preparing to activate your New Moon dream! Allow yourself plenty of time to play with this!

Review the possibility you decided to activate during this lunar cycle and write a creation statement (an intention) to activate more VIBRANT HEALTH. Remember your statement is to be in the present and not in the future!

_____

OK, Dear Heart, now let's turn that intention into a goal with 3 actionable steps!

3 actions I am taking in the next two weeks to manifest more VIBRANT HEALTH.

_____
_____
_____

Awesome! You now have a goal and 3 actionable steps to take!

Here's the next part of your New Moon Creation Ceremony! We invite you to create a mini angel board! It's a vision board with the Angels! On your paper using your pens and markers write your intention and the 3 actions you are taking in the next two weeks!

Be sure to write Thank You on your board. You can write a simple Thank You or something more elaborate, "Thank You Angels and Lady Luna for this and all deliciousness I'm creating now!"

Be creative! Create something you'd like to look at least once a day, each and EVERY day! Make it fun … catchy … playful!!

When you've completed your mini angel board put your tools away.

Thank Archangel Gabriel and Lady Luna and extinguish your candle.

Be sure to place your Angel Board where you will see it every day for the next two weeks!

Here are some things you might like to do to keep your mini angel board in your awareness:

- Take a picture on your phone and make it your screen saver.
- Take a photo on your computer and make it your screen saver.
- Frame it and put it on your desk or in your kitchen.
- Keep it on your bed stand. It's great seeing it first thing in the morning and again just before falling asleep!

Dear Heart, FOLLOW YOUR ACTIONABLE STEPS! When you DO something toward your goals you are actually creating an energetic alignment. And you know alignment helps you manifest more quickly!

MAY

may

S	M	T	W	T	F	S
					1	2
3	4	5	6	7	8	9
10	11	12	13	14	15	16
17	18	19	20	21	22	23
24	25	26	27	28	29	30
31						

notes

21 THURSDAY	**22** FRIDAY	**23** SATURDAY	**24** SUNDAY
	NEW MOON ASTRO SIGN: GEMINI ANGEL CODES: 4/2		

MAY

may

S	M	T	W	T	F	S
					1	2
3	4	5	6	7	8	9
10	11	12	13	14	15	16
17	18	19	20	21	22	23
24	25	26	27	28	29	30
31						

notes

25 MONDAY

26 TUESDAY

27 WEDNESDAY

28 THURSDAY	29 FRIDAY	30 SATURDAY	31 SUNDAY

June 2020 Overlighting Angel Code 10 | Gateway to The Universal Light Star

Activation: Activates Light unifying your physical Body Temple with your Light Body, Divine Light of the Universe and all Benevolent Light Beings.

The angels are reminding you that you are a Light Being living in a physical human body. Here, they connect you to the Divine Light of the Universe and all Light Beings as they align your physical body with your Light Body. Do not hide your light beneath the barrel. Shine Bright Dear One!

ARCHANGEL ARIEL'S MESSAGE 10 | GATEWAY TO THE UNIVERSAL LIGHT STAR

Dear One, here we have the energetic signature of the Universal Light Star aligning you with all the light of the universe ... for you are a Divine Light Star. It's who you are Dear One. You hold the light of the universe. You are a star that shines brighter than your sun ... brighter than the fixed star Sirius. Your light holds the codes of the universe's energetic signatures just as your water holds the codes of your spiritual DNA and your bones hold the codes of the cosmic crystals. How perfectly delightful that this is the angel code for June, a month of much light!

JUNE ANGEL MANTRA

🦋 *"As I Shine my Divine Light, I resonate Love and Grace. I become a beacon of Grace for others."*

THIS MONTH'S ANGEL MANTRA ACTIVATION

Each morning this month, look into a mirror, begin taking long, slow, deep breaths all the way into your belly. As you breathe, bring your awareness into your SoulHeart. Feel your beautiful SoulHeart expanding. Feel the shift. Do you feel warm... or cool? Do you feel vibration? See color? Now, bring your awareness back to your breath and take 3 long, slow, deep breaths. On each outbreath, repeat or tone the Angel Mantra out loud.

🦋 *"As I Shine my Divine Light, I resonate Love and Grace. I become a beacon of Grace for others."*

Repeat for a total of 3 breaths. For an even deeper alignment, repeat this in the evenings, too!

june

SUNDAY	MONDAY	TUESDAY
	1	2
7	8	9
14	15	16
21 NEW MOON ECLIPSE (CANCER) ANGEL CODES: 4/0	22	23
28	29	30

This Month

_____

_____

_____

_____

_____

_____

_____

_____

_____

_____

_____

_____

_____

2020

WEDNESDAY	THURSDAY	FRIDAY	SATURDAY
3	4	5 FULL MOON ECLIPSE (SAGITTARIUS) ANGEL CODES: 6/6	6
10	11	12	13
17	18	19 MERCURY RETROGRADE	20 SOLSTICE *SOLAR ECLIPSE BEGINS*
24	25	26	27

June Full Moon Lunar Eclipse

DATE: FRIDAY, JUNE 5 / LUNATION: 12:44 AM (NEW YORK)
ASTRO SIGN: 15° SAGITTARIUS / RULER: JUPITER
ELEMENT: FIRE / EXPRESSION: MUTABLE
ARCHANGEL: URIEL

FULL MOON KEYWORDS: COMPLETION, SURRENDER

ECLIPSES

This penumbral lunar eclipse occurring at the end of Spring is the second eclipse of 2020! Eclipses usually come in pairs and activate a particular axis (astrological signs that are opposite each other). This eclipse in Sagittarius activates the Gemini/Sagittarius Axis. Eclipses amplify the lunar energies about three times more than a non-eclipse moon!

LUNA'S ASTRO ENERGIES

Lady Luna brings this lunar eclipse in Jupiter ruled Sagittarius, the happiest sign in the zodiac! When Luna shines her Sagittarian light, she is generous, idealistic and open-minded. She loves her freedom, the wind in her hair and exploring new places! During this portal of surrender you're invited to surrender anything that keeps you from expressing Sagittarian qualities! Is there some place in your life where you don't believe "the universe will provide"? If so, that might be a place to surrender!

JUNE 5 SAGITTARIUS FULL MOON ANGEL CODES 6/6

This Full Moon Eclipse activates the energetic signature of ANGEL CODE 6/6.

OVERLIGHTING and LUNATION ANGEL CODE 6 | GATEWAY OF INFINITE KNOWING
Activation: Activates your intuition in all realms and dimensions.

Darling Heart, how powerful this is! BOTH the Overlighting Angel Code and the Lunation Angel Code are 6 … and June is the 6th month … and of course, the Sun is also activating this code! The angels are inviting you to pay attention! This Angel Code of Infinite Knowing is amplified FOUR times!!!

ARCHANGEL ARIEL'S MESSAGE 6 | GATEWAY OF INFINITE KNOWING

Dear One, remember you are a masterful intuitive being. You are not of the Earth. Yet part of you is in your Earth Body … There is so much more. You are a masterful intuitive and as you awaken, you will tune into the infinite knowing … unexpected at first and then proceeding at will. Opening the Gateway of Infinite Knowing connects you to the Whole of Life and the Whole of Your Being! Do you see? You are receiving this message tri-fold today!

JUNE 5 SAGITTARIUS FULL MOON ACTIVATION FOR MATERIAL WEALTH

Full Moon activates completion and surrendering things in your life that no longer serve. And, of course, Darling Heart, always surrender with love and gratitude! This Full Moon Eclipse you have the powerful support of Archangel Uriel and Lady Luna in her Sagittarian energies as you are invited for the second time this year to surrender blocks to Material Wealth!

Please take some quiet time this week feeling into the **Angel Code 6 | Gateway Of Infinite Knowing**. Feel into **Lady Luna's Astro Energies of Jupiter ruled Sagittarius**. Here Luna is on fire and ready to ignite your dreams of Wealth. Riding tandem with beneficent Jupiter it's time to release your blocks to prosperity. How can you use these energies to help you surrender blocks to MATERIAL WEALTH?

Darling Heart, we invite you to spend some quiet time on Friday tuning into your beautiful Infinite Heart, feeling into your dreams and wishes. Feeling into Love. On this Full Moon decide on one thing you want to surrender that you believe is keeping your Heart from experiencing its most delicious Joy. To help you sort it out, call on Archangel Uriel, Angel of Sagittarius, Angel of Light and Clarity. Here's our checklist:

Material Wealth
On a scale of 1 – 10, what's your number? _____
(10 feeling absolutely divinely Wealthy, 1 wondering how you are going to pay your bills).

Darling Heart, come to stillness and feel into your relationship with Money. Here are some common thoughts associated with money. Check those that apply.

How I Feel About My Money
I love having enough money to do all the things I love without ever having to think about how much it cost. _____
I just don't have enough for lot of extras. ____
I get a knot in my belly/ heart rate shifts when I think about money. __

<u>Savings</u>

I pay my savings account first. _____

I put money in my savings account every week/paycheck/month. _____

I have a retirement plan. ____

I don't have a solid plan. _____

I live from paycheck to paycheck. ____

<u>Purchases</u>

I love new clothes and buy cute things when I see them. _____

I can afford the things I want (gym/classes/conferences/vacations/travel). __

I rarely buy anything new. _____

<u>Credit Cards</u>

I use my charge accounts and pay them off every month._____

I use my charge accounts and carry a balance. _____

I use my charge cards and pay the minimum each month. ____

Look at what you've written and name one thing you are willing to surrender this Full Moon to that you believe blocks your Material Wealth.

_____

_____

JUNE 5 SAGITTARIUS FULL MOON FIRE CEREMONY OF SURRENDER

Gather Your Sacred Tools:

- 🦅 The Angel Code Oracle 2020
- 🦅 A candle and lighter
- 🦅 A fireproof bowl
- 🦅 A small piece of paper for burning
- 🦅 A pen or pencil

Dear One, go to a space where you won't be disturbed and light your candle. Call in Archangel Uriel to help you come fully into your shining heart as you release with love and gratitude. Write whatever you are surrendering on a small slip of paper. Read what you've written out loud. You might use these words:

"By the light of this full moon I surrender _____to the Sacred Fires. I surrender with Love and Gratitude and I am now complete with _____."

Then light your paper and watch it burn. Knowing you have surrendered, released and are now complete. Sit for a moment. Feel into the power of surrender. And now write whatever impressions, feelings and awareness you have.

_____

_____

_____

Thank Archangel Uriel and Lady Luna and extinguish your fire.

What to do with the ashes? Many people choose to bury them. I like to go outside by the light of the moon, hold the ashes in my palm and blow them away!

Darling Heart, a surrendering ceremony is really powerful …trust that whatever you have released no longer has power over you and be sure not to re-invoke it into your life!

JUNE

june

S	M	T	W	T	F	S
	1	2	3	4	5	6
7	8	9	10	11	12	13
14	15	16	17	18	19	20
21	22	23	24	25	26	27
28	29	30				

notes

1 MONDAY	2 TUESDAY	3 WEDNESDAY

4 THURSDAY	**5** FRIDAY	**6** SATURDAY	**7** SUNDAY
	FULL MOON *PENUMBRAL LUNAR ECLIPSE* ASTRO SIGN: SAGITTARIUS ANGEL CODES: 6/6		

JUNE

june

S	M	T	W	T	F	S
		1	2	3	4	5	6
7	8	9	10	11	12	13
14	15	16	17	18	19	20
21	22	23	24	25	26	27
28	29	30				

notes

8 MONDAY	**9** TUESDAY	**10** WEDNESDAY

11 THURSDAY	12 FRIDAY	13 SATURDAY	14 SUNDAY

June New Moon Solar Eclipse

DATE: SUNDAY, JUNE 21 / LUNATION: 2:42 AM (NEW YORK)
ASTRO SIGN: 0° CANCER / RULER: MOON
ELEMENT: WATER / EXPRESSION: CARDINAL
ARCHANGEL: RAPHAEL

NEW MOON KEYWORDS: NEW BEGINNINGS, CREATION

ECLIPSES

This annular solar eclipse is the first solar eclipse of the year, the third eclipse of 2020 and the first of our Summer Eclipse Season. Eclipses usually come in pairs and activate a particular axis (astrological signs that are opposite each other). This eclipse is the second Cancer eclipse this year and activates the Cancer/ Capricorn Axis. Eclipses amplify the lunar energies about three times more than a non-eclipse moon!

LUNA'S ASTRO ENERGIES

This solar eclipse happens in the first new moon in our new season, Summer. Lady Luna is in her home sign of Cancer where she has opened the doorway to a new beginning in a new season. OMGoddess. New season, new moon, solar eclipse in her own sign! How powerful is that! You're invited to create in the place of your heart … where is your heart at home? Who do you love as family? When Lady Luna is in her sign of cancer she creates through emotion. What do your emotions motivate you to create? Create Heart inspired deliciousness!

JUNE 21 CANCER NEW MOON ANGEL CODE 4/0

OVERLIGHTING ANGEL CODE 4 | GATEWAY TO THE INFINITE HEART
Activation: Activating your Light of Infinite Love shining through your Infinite SoulHeart.

Darling Heart, the angels are reminding you that you are a Being of Infinite Love shining through your infinite heart.

ARCHANGEL ARIEL'S MESSAGE 4 | GATEWAY TO THE INFINTE HEART

Remember Dear One, you are a divine being choosing a life in the physical form. It is your Infinite Soul Heart that is meant to guide you. For you are meant to live on your planet as a divine being experiencing the most delicious life you can imagine. Remember, Dear One, only a portion of your divine being is within your physical form. You have many waiting to serve you ... Angels, guides, ascended masters, cosmic being ... Your connection to all of your soul gifts and talents is through your magnificent heart. Let your heart be your guide. When things feel resonant, move forward. When you are feeling discord, retreat. Allow your awareness of your SoulHeart frequency to grow. When you are not sure, feel into your precious SoulHeart. Ask questions. Feel into your heart. You will become more skilled as you practice.

LUNATION ANGEL CODE 0 | GATEWAY OF THE SACRED MOTHERS
Activation: Activates the union of Divine Mother and Earth Mother through two grids; the Sacred Water Grid and the Sacred Crystal Grid.

This angel code holds the energetic signature of eternity, the zero point, always flowing, never ending. The angels are offering you this circle of eternity unifying The Sacred Mothers of Earth and Cosmos through water and crystal. This code is amplified because the Sun is also activating 0!

ARCHANGEL ARIEL'S MESSAGE 0 | GATEWAY OF THE SACRED MOTHERS

You are a magnificent cosmic being, a glowing orb of divine light and energy who has chosen to bring part of yourself into physical form. And yet, even your physical form holds your divine essence ... You hold the sacred grids of water and crystal within you ... The spiritual DNA in the cosmic waters flows through your bodies nourishing and replenishing every cell and every tissue as the crystals making up your bone structures nourish and replenish your blood. And the circle remains unbroken.

JUNE 21 CANCER NEW MOON ACTIVATION FOR MATERIAL WEALTH

New Moon activates new beginnings, visioning, setting goals and creating while you have the powerful support of Archangel Raphael and Lady Luna. On the last Full Moon, you were invited to surrender something that blocks your MATERIAL WEALTH so now, on this New Moon, we invite you for the second time to create more wealth in your life!

As we move through the Wheel of the Year, this New Moon is the second time we are inviting you to manifest MATERIAL WEALTH!

Please take some quiet time this week feeling into the **Angel Codes 4 | Gateway To The Infinite Heart** and **0 | Gateway Of The Sacred Mothers.** Feel into **Lady Luna's Astro Energies of Moon ruled Cancer.** Here Luna is in her Watery native energies... she rules the tides and your emotions! She rules home and family. How can you use these energies to help you create more MATERIAL WEALTH?

Darling Heart, we invite you to spend some quiet time on Sunday tuning into your beautiful Infinite Heart, feeling into your dreams and wishes around your Wealth. Call on Archangel Raphael the

Angel of Cancer, Angel of Love, Healing and Forgiveness to help you create a change activating more MATERIAL WEALTH!

Sweet One, ask yourself the following question:

Material Wealth
On a scale of 1 – 10 What's your number? _____
(10 feeling absolutely divinely wealthy, 1 wondering how you are going to pay your bills.)

And now, come to stillness and feel into your relationship with Money. Here are some common thoughts associated with money. Check those that apply:

How I Feel About My Money
I love having enough money to do all the things I love without ever having to think about
    how much it cost. _____
I just don't have enough for lots of extras. ____
I get a knot in my belly/ heart rate shifts when I think about money. __

Savings
I pay my savings account first. _____
I put money in my savings account every week/paycheck/month. _____
I have a retirement plan. ____
I don't have a solid plan. __
I live from paycheck to paycheck. ____

Purchases
I love new clothes and buy cute things when I see them. _____
I can afford the things I want (gym/classes/conferences/vacations/travel). __
I rarely buy anything new. _____

Credit Cards
I use my charge accounts and pay them off every month. _____
I use my charge accounts and carry a balance. _____
I use my charge cards and pay the minimum each month. ____

From the list above write down 3 possible ways you can create even more MATERIAL WEALTH.

_____
_____
_____

Read each possibility out loud. Feel into them. Does one stand out from the other two? Does one bring a smile as you read it? Is one easier to manifest? Or do you feel the timing is right... Or not?

Which possibility on your list of 3 is the one to activate during this lunar cycle?

_____

JUNE 21 CANCER NEW MOON CEREMONY OF CREATION

Gather Your Sacred Tools:

- 🦋 The Angel Code Oracle 2020
- 🦋 A candle and lighter
- 🦋 Paper, pens, markers etc.
- 🦋 A pen or pencil

Sweet One, go to a space where you won't be disturbed and light your candle. Call in Archangel Raphael to help inspire you as you come fully into your shining heart preparing to activate your New Moon dream! Allow yourself plenty of time to play with this!

Review the possibility you decided to activate during this lunar cycle and write a creation statement (an intention) to activate more Material Wealth. Remember your statement is to be in the present and not in the future!

_____

OK, Dear Heart, now let's turn that intention into a goal with 3 actionable steps!

3 actions I am taking in the next two weeks to manifest more MATERIAL WEALTH!

_____
_____
_____

Awesome! You now have a goal and 3 actionable steps to take!

Here's the next part of your New Moon Creation Ceremony! We invite you to create a mini angel board! It's a vision board with the Angels! On your paper using your pens and markers write your intention and the 3 actions you are taking in the next two weeks!

Be sure to write Thank You on your board. You can write a simple Thank You or something more elaborate, "Thank You Angels and Lady Luna for this and all deliciousness I'm creating now!"

Be creative! Create something you'd like to look at least once a day, each and EVERY day! Make it fun … catchy … playful!!

When you've completed your mini angel board put your tools away.

Thank Archangel Raphael and Lady Luna and extinguish your candle.

Be sure to place your Angel Board where you will see it every day for the next two weeks!

Here are some things you might like to do to keep your mini angel board in your awareness:

- Take a picture on your phone and make it your screen saver.
- Take a photo on your computer and make it your screen saver.
- Frame it and put it on your desk or in your kitchen.
- Keep it on your bed stand. It's great seeing it first thing in the morning and again just before falling asleep!

Dear Heart, FOLLOW YOUR ACTIONABLE STEPS! When you DO something toward your goals you are actually creating an energetic alignment. And you know alignment helps you manifest more quickly!

JUNE

june

S	M	T	W	T	F	S
		1	2	3	4	5	6
7	8	9	10	11	12	13
14	15	16	17	18	19	20
21	22	23	24	25	26	27
28	29	30				

notes

15 MONDAY	**16** TUESDAY	**17** WEDNESDAY

18 THURSDAY	19 FRIDAY	20 SATURDAY	21 SUNDAY
	MERCURY RETROGRADE	SOLSTICE *ANNULAR SOLAR ECLIPSE BEGINS*	NEW MOON *ANNULAR SOLAR ECLIPSE* ASTRO SIGN: CANCER ANGEL CODES: 4/0

JUNE

june

S	M	T	W	T	F	S
	1	2	3	4	5	6
7	8	9	10	11	12	13
14	15	16	17	18	19	20
21	22	23	24	25	26	27
28	29	30				

notes

22 MONDAY	23 TUESDAY	24 WEDNESDAY

25 THURSDAY	**26** FRIDAY	**27** SATURDAY	**28** SUNDAY

July 2020 Overlighting Angel Code
11 | Gateway to The Galaxies

Activation: Activates your expansion of consciousness to travel beyond time and space.

This month's Overlighting Angel Code invites you to expand your consciousness, surrender limitations and journey beyond time and space. Angels invite you to understand clocks are an agreement made by society to keep things running smoothly in the everyday … Angels invite you to play with time and space. Stay fully present in the moment … in that place of no time and no space … Stay in the knowing that there is no time nor space beyond the present.

ARCHANGEL ARIEL'S MESSAGE 11 | GATEWAY TO THE GALAXIES

And so, Dear One, here we have the activation of the code 11 the Galactic Gateway. Dear One, you are a limitless being._Your natural state of being knows no boundaries … Knows no clocks … No should … No color within the lines. There is limitless freedom as you allow yourself to experience your Galactic self! Sing … Dance … Drum … Jump timelines! As was written in an earth song "We are Stardust" and so you are.

ANGEL MANTRA

- ❦ *"I am limitless. I am Stardust. When I am in the Now, I enjoy magical moments!"*

THIS MONTH'S ANGEL MANTRA ACTIVATION

Each morning look into a mirror. Begin taking long, slow, deep breaths all the way into your belly. As you breathe bring your awareness into your SoulHeart. Feel your beautiful SoulHeart expanding. Feel the shift. Do you feel warm … or cool? Do you feel vibration? See color? Now, bring your awareness back to your breath and take 3 long, slow, deep breaths. On each outbreath, repeat or tone the Angel Mantra out loud.

- ❦ *"I am limitless. I am Stardust. When I am in the Now, I enjoy magical moments!"*

Repeat for a total of 3 breaths. For an even deeper alignment, repeat this in the evenings too!

july

SUNDAY	MONDAY	TUESDAY
5 **FULL MOON ECLIPSE (CAPRICORN)** ANGEL CODES: 7/4	6	7
12	13	14
19	20 **NEW MOON (CANCER)** ANGEL CODES: 4/10	21
26	27	28

2020

WEDNESDAY	THURSDAY	FRIDAY	SATURDAY
1	2	3	4 LUNAR ECLIPSE BEGINS
8	9	10	11 MERCURY DIRECT
15	16	17	18
22	23	24	25
29	30	31	

July Full Moon Lunar Eclipse

DATE: SUNDAY, JULY 5 / LUNATION: 12:44 AM (NEW YORK)
ASTRO SIGN: 13° CAPRICORN / RULER: SATURN
ELEMENT: EARTH / EXPRESSION: CARDINAL
ARCHANGEL: MICHAEL

FULL MOON KEYWORDS: COMPLETION, SURRENDER

ECLIPSES

This fourth penumbral lunar eclipse is our second and final eclipse of the 2020 Summer Eclipse Season. Eclipses usually come in pairs and activate a particular axis (astrological signs that are opposite each other). This eclipse in the sign of Capricorn activates the Cancer/Capricorn Axis. Eclipses amplify the lunar energies about three times more than a non-eclipse moon!

LUNA'S ASTRO ENERGIES

When Lady Luna is shining her Capricorn light, she activates the energetic signature of the leader! Responsible, divinely disciplined with ease and self-control this magical mountain goat can manage anything! In this portal of surrender Lady Luna is inviting you to let go of anything you have already completed and anything that keeps you from being the natural born leader you are meant to be!

JULY 5 CAPRICORN FULL MOON ANGEL CODE 7/4

This Full Moon Eclipse activates the energetic signature of Angel Code 7/4.

OVERLIGHTING ANGEL CODE 7 | GATEWAY TO THE DIVINE COLLECTIVE
Activation: Activates your connection to the Collective Consciousness

The Angel Code 7 activates the energetic signature of the Collective Consciousness! Here, you are reminded that you are a being of Divine Energy. You are part of the Divine Collective. Your thoughts and actions are energy forms that affect the whole of life … even the weather!

ARCHANGEL ARIEL'S MESSAGE 7 | GATEWAY TO THE DIVINE COLLECTIVE

Dear One, we invite you to awaken to the knowledge that All Are One. There is a collective … no separation. You are part of the Whole. What you do, what you say, and what you think affects the Whole of Life… not just beings who breathe but the mountains, seas, waters, weather. All are a reflection of the energetic signature sent forth. Do you believe the words you speak are just words. Or do you understand the power they hold? You are a powerful creator! Once you breathe life into your words by speaking them aloud you have set a powerful invocation. You have released the energetic signature of those words into the universe. And the energy will build as it gathers more energy that is in vibrational coherence with its energetic signatures. Dear One, by the words you speak you can create Peace, Love, Kindness and Happiness in the collective or you can create War, Destruction, Disease and Divisiveness. What you create affects the whole of humanity. Keep your thoughts uplifted. Treat others with respect. Care for your planet. Understand All Are One and YOU affect the Whole! Now that you hold this understanding, we know you will create from your Divine SoulHeart.

LUNATION ANGEL CODE 4 | GATEWAY TO THE INFINITE HEART
Activation: Activating your Light of Infinite Love shining through your Infinite SoulHeart.

The angels are reminding you that you are a Being of Infinite Love shining through your Infinite SoulHeart. This Code is amplified because the Sun is activating 4!

ARCHANGEL ARIEL'S MESSAGE 4 | GATEWAY TO THE INFINITE HEART

Remember Dear One, you are a divine being choosing a life in the physical form. It is your Infinite SoulHeart that is meant to guide you. For you are meant to live on your planet as a divine being experiencing the most delicious life you can imagine. Remember, Dear One, only a portion of your divine being is within your physical form. You have many waiting to serve you … Angels, guides, ascended masters, cosmic beings … Your connection to all of your soul gifts and talents is through your magnificent heart. Let your heart be your guide. When things feel resonant move forward. When you are feeling discord, retreat. Allow your awareness of your SoulHeart frequency to grow. When you are not sure, feel into your Infinite SoulHeart. Ask questions. Feel into your heart. You will become more skilled as you practice.

JULY 5 CAPRICORN FULL MOON ACTIVATION FOR LOVE

Full Moons activate completion and surrendering things in your life that no longer serve a purpose. And, of course, Sweet One, always surrender with love and gratitude. You now have the powerful support of Archangel Michael and Lady Luna in her Capricorn energies. This Full Moon you are invited for the third time this year to surrender blocks to Love!

Please take some quiet time this week feeling into the **Angel Codes 7 | Gateway To The Divine Collective** and **4 | Gateway To The Infinite Heart.** Feel into **Lady Luna's Astro Energies of Saturn ruled Capricorn.** Here earthy Luna is responsible, divinely disciplined with ease and self-control. This magical mountain goat can manage anything. How can you use these energies to help you surrender blocks to LOVE?

Darling Heart, we invite you to spend some quiet time on Sunday tuning into your beautiful Infinite Heart, feeling into your dreams and wishes. Feeling into Love. On this Full Moon, the third Full Moon opportunity to surrender blocks to Love, decide on one thing you want to surrender that you believe is keeping your Heart from experiencing its most delicious Joy. To help you sort it out, call on Archangel Michael the angel of Capricorn, angel of strength and courage to bring you strength and courage as you surrender blocks to LOVE! Dear One, here are some things to consider:

What is your passion? _____

_____

What makes your heart sing? _____

_____

Are you expressing too much self-control when it comes to Love? no__ yes__

What earthy deliciousness do you absolutely love?
    drumming__ walking barefoot in the moonlight__ camping__ playing in forests__
    lying in a field under the night sky__ other_____

BONUS QUESTION
On a scale of 1-10 How much do you love yourself? What's your number? _____
(10 is *Yes! I'm absolutely, totally awesome!* 1 is *I'm a mess. Totally unworthy of love.*)

If you rated yourself less than 10, what is keeping you from absolutely adoring your totally awesome self? _____

Look at what you've written and create one thing you are willing to surrender that you believe blocks LOVE in your life.

_____

JULY 5 CAPRICORN FULL MOON FIRE CEREMONY OF SURRENDER

Gather Your Sacred Tools:

- The Angel Code Oracle 2020
- A candle and lighter
- A fireproof bowl
- A small piece of paper for burning
- A pen or pencil

Go to a space where you won't be disturbed and light your candle. Call in Archangel Michael to help you come fully into your shining heart as you release with love and gratitude. Write whatever you are surrendering on a small slip of paper. Read what you've written out loud. You might use these words:

"By the light of this full moon I surrender _____to the Sacred Fires. I surrender with Love and Gratitude and I am now complete with _____."

Then light your paper and watch it burn. Knowing you have surrendered, released and are now complete. Sit for a moment. Feel into the power of surrender. And now write whatever impressions, feelings and awareness you have. _____
_____
_____
_____

Thank Archangel Michael and Lady Luna and extinguish your fire.

What to do with the ashes? Many people choose to bury them. I like to go outside by the light of the moon, hold the ashes in my palm and blow them away!

Darling Heart, a surrendering ceremony is really powerful…trust that whatever you have released no longer has power over you and be sure not to re-invoke it into your life!

Yoo-hoo! Angel Code Oracle 2021 is in production...

We're pleased to announce THE ANGEL CODE ORACLE 2021 is in production! Have you signed up for the waitlist, yet? It's easy. Just send an e-mail to:
Taco2021waitlist@katebeloved.com

We'll send an e-mail as soon as it's available!

We know you're creating an amazing year!
Abundant Angel Blessings
Beloveds

JULY

july

S	M	T	W	T	F	S
		1	2	3	4	
5	6	7	8	9	10	11
12	13	14	15	16	17	18
19	20	21	22	23	24	25
26	27	28	29	30	31	

notes

29	30	1
MONDAY	TUESDAY	WEDNESDAY

2 THURSDAY	3 FRIDAY	4 SATURDAY	5 SUNDAY
		PRENUMBRAL LUNAR ECLIPSE BEGINS	FULL MOON *PENUMBRAL LUNAR ECLIPSE* ASTRO SIGN: CAPRICORN ANGEL CODES: 7/4

JULY

july

S	M	T	W	T	F	S
			1	2	3	4
5	6	7	8	9	10	11
12	13	14	15	16	17	18
19	20	21	22	23	24	25
26	27	28	29	30	31	

notes

6 MONDAY	**7** TUESDAY	**8** WEDNESDAY

9 THURSDAY	10 FRIDAY	11 SATURDAY	12 SUNDAY
		MERCURY DIRECT	

JULY

july

S	M	T	W	T	F	S
		1	2	3	4	
5	6	7	8	9	10	11
12	13	14	15	16	17	18
19	20	21	22	23	24	25
26	27	28	29	30	31	

notes

13 MONDAY	**14** TUESDAY	**15** WEDNESDAY

16 THURSDAY	17 FRIDAY	18 SATURDAY	19 SUNDAY

July New Moon

DATE: MONDAY, JULY 20 / LUNATION: 1:33 PM (NEW YORK)
ASTRO SIGN: 28° CANCER / RULER: MOON
ELEMENT: WATER / EXPRESSION: CARDINAL
ARCHANGEL: RAPHAEL

NEW MOON KEYWORDS: NEW BEGINNING, CREATION

LUNA'S ASTRO ENERGIES

Oh, My Darling Heart, this is our SECOND new moon in Cancer! Last month our New Moon Solar Eclipse on June 21st lunation was at 0° Cancer. When things repeat it's the universe's way of saying, "PAY ATTENTION!" Once again, you're being invited to create your heart's desire! How awesome is that! When Lady Luna is shining her Cancerian light, she is highlighting home and family. I invite you to tune into your Infinite Heart. Where does your beautiful SoulHeart feel "at home"? Who is your Heart family? Create Heart inspired deliciousness!

JULY 20 CANCER NEW MOON ANGEL CODE 4/10

OVERLIGHTING ANGEL CODE 4 | GATEWAY TO THE INFINITE HEART
Activation: Activating your Light of Infinite Love shining through your Infinite SoulHeart.

The angels are reminding you that you are a being of infinite love shining through your infinite heart.

ARCHANGEL ARIEL'S MESSAGE 4 | GATEWAY TO THE INFINITE HEART

Remember Dear One, you are a divine being choosing a life in the physical form. It is your Infinite SoulHeart that is meant to guide you. For you are meant to live on your planet as a divine being experiencing the most delicious life you can imagine. Remember, dear one, only a portion of your divine being is within your physical form. You have many waiting to serve you… Angels, guides, ascended masters, cosmic beings … Your connection to all of your soul gifts and talents is through your magnificent heart. Let your heart be your guide. When things feel resonant, move forward. When you are feeling discord, retreat. Allow your awareness of your SoulHeart frequency to grow. When you are not sure, feel into your precious SoulHeart. Ask questions. Feel into your heart. You will become more skilled as you practice.

LUNATION ANGEL CODE 10 | GATEWAY OF THE UNIVERSAL LIGHT STAR
Activation: Activates Light unifying your physical Body Temple with your Light Body, Divine Light of the Universe and all Benevolent Light Beings.

The angels are reminding you that you are a Light Being living in a physical human body. Here, they connect you to the Divine Light of the Universe and all Light Beings as they align your physical body with your Light Body. Do not hide your light beneath the barrel … Shine Bright Dear One!

ARCHANGEL ARIEL'S MESSAGE 10 | GATEWAY OF THE UNIVERSAL LIGHT STAR

Dear One, Angel Code 10 brings light from the universe into your physical body. Light holds the divine spark … light is energy. Energy of the universe is pouring through your physical body temple merging spirit into matter … illuminating your brilliant Self!

JULY 20 CANCER NEW MOON ACTIVATION FOR LOVE

New Moon activates new beginnings, visioning, setting goals and creating while you have the powerful support of Archangel Raphael and Lady Luna. As we move through the Wheel of the Year, this New Moon is the third New Moon inviting you to focus on manifesting more LOVE in your life!

Please take some quiet time this week feeling into the **Angel Codes 4 | Gateway To The Infinite Heart** and **10 | Gateway Of The Universal Light Star.** Feel into **Lady Luna's Astro Energies of Moon ruled Cancer.** Here Luna is in her Watery native energies… she rules the tides and your emotions! She rules home and family. How can these energies help you activate more LOVE?

Darling Heart, we invite you to spend some quiet time on Monday tuning into your beautiful Infinite Heart, feeling into your dreams and wishes. Feeling into Love. Call on Archangel Raphael, Angel of Cancer, Angel of Love, Healing and Forgiveness to be with you supporting you as you manifest more LOVE.

And now, Sweet One, ask yourself the following questions:

What is your passion? _____

_____

What makes your heart sing? _____

_____

Where does your Infinite Heart feel at home? _____

_____

Who do you call family? _____
_____

How can you bring more of that into your life during this Lunar cycle? _____
_____

From the above questions write down 3 dreams to create more LOVE in your life.
_____
_____
_____

Read each dream out loud. Feel into them. Does one stand out from the other two? Does one bring a smile as you read it? Is one easier to manifest? Or do you feel the timing is right… Or not?

Which dream on your list of 3 is the one to activate during this lunar cycle?
_____

JULY 20 CANCER NEW MOON CEREMONY OF CREATION

Gather Your Sacred Tools:

- The Angel Code Oracle 2020
- A candle and lighter
- Paper, pens, markers etc.
- A pen or pencil

Sweet One, go to a space where you won't be disturbed and light your candle. Call in Archangel Raphael to help inspire you as you come fully into your shining heart preparing to activate your New Moon dream! Allow yourself plenty of time to play with this!

Review the dream you decided to activate during this lunar cycle and write a creation statement (an intention) to create more LOVE in your life. Remember your statement is to be in the present and not in the future!
_____
_____

OK, Dear Heart, now let's turn that intention into a goal with 3 actionable steps!

3 Actions I am taking in the next two weeks to manifest my intention and bring more delicious LOVE in my life!

_____

_____

_____

Awesome! You now have a goal and 3 actionable steps to take!

Here's the next part of your New Moon Creation Ceremony! We invite you to create a mini angel board! It's a vision board with the Angels! On your paper using your pens and markers write your intention and the 3 actions you are taking in the next two weeks!

Be sure to write Thank You on your board. You can write a simple Thank You or something more elaborate, "Thank You Angels and Lady Luna for this and all deliciousness I'm creating now!"

Be creative! Create something you'd like to look at least once a day, each and EVERY day! Make it fun … catchy … playful!!

When you've completed your mini angel board put your tools away.

Thank Archangel Raphael and Lady Luna and extinguish your candle.

Be sure to place your Angel Board where you will see it every day for the next two weeks!

Here are some things you might like to do to keep your mini angel board in your awareness:

- Take a picture on your phone and make it your screen saver.
- Take a photo on your computer and make it your screen saver.
- Frame it and put it on your desk or in your kitchen.
- Keep it on your bed stand. It's great seeing it first thing in the morning and again just before falling asleep!

Dear Heart, FOLLOW YOUR ACTIONABLE STEPS! When you DO something toward your goals you are actually creating an energetic alignment. And you know alignment helps you manifest more quickly!

JULY

july

S	M	T	W	T	F	S
			1	2	3	4
5	6	7	8	9	10	11
12	13	14	15	16	17	18
19	20	21	22	23	24	25
26	27	28	29	30	31	

notes

20
MONDAY

NEW MOON
ASTRO SIGN: CANCER
ANGEL CODES: 4/10

21
TUESDAY

22
WEDNESDAY

23 THURSDAY	**24** FRIDAY	**25** SATURDAY	**26** SUNDAY

JULY

july

S	M	T	W	T	F	S
			1	2	3	4
5	6	7	8	9	10	11
12	13	14	15	16	17	18
19	20	21	22	23	24	25
26	27	28	29	30	31	

notes

27 MONDAY	28 TUESDAY	29 WEDNESDAY

30 THURSDAY	31 FRIDAY	1 SATURDAY	2 SUNDAY

August 2020 Overlighting Angel Code 12 | Gateway to The Heart of The Divine Mother

Activation: Activates direct connection to the Divine through the Divine Mother Essence.

The Overlighting Angel Code for August 2020 activates direct connection to the Divine through the essence of the Divine Mother.

ARCHANGEL ARIEL'S MESSAGE 12 | GATEWAY TO THE HEART OF THE DIVINE MOTHER

Here we have the energetic signature of the Divine Mother… the essence of divinity of The All… of God, Goddess, Creator, Source, however you understand THE ONE. Understand this energy not as a mother you have known in physical form, but as a Divine Mother who comes in with the energetic signature of the Divine Creator and invites you to be open to the qualities of the Divine Feminine … to understand that your world must now live through the SoulHeart. To live the qualities of the empowered mother… of divine feminine …. Those qualities of unconditional love … of honoring … cooperation … respect … and allowing others to be what they are meant to be … to live their lives following their own paths … and to live your earth journey in your way … knowing that you are a multidimensional Divine Spiritual Being. Through the frequencies of the Divine Mother essence you are also connected to all essences of the divine … you are one with Divine Energy.

AUGUST ANGEL MANTRA

🕊 *"I am a multi-dimensional Divine Spiritual Being. I am Divine Mother essence."*

THIS MONTH'S ANGEL MANTRA ACTIVATION

Each morning, look into a mirror, begin taking long, slow, deep breaths all the way into your belly. As you breathe bring your awareness into your SoulHeart. Feel your beautiful SoulHeart expanding. Feel the shift. Do you feel warm … or cool? Do you feel vibration? See color? Now, bring your awareness back to your breath and take 3 long, slow, deep breaths. On each outbreath repeat or tone the Angel Mantra out loud:

🕊 *"I am a multi-dimensional Divine Spiritual Being. I am Divine Mother essence".*

Repeat for a total of 3 breaths. For an even deeper alignment, repeat this in the evenings too!

august

	SUNDAY	MONDAY	TUESDAY
This Month			
	2	3 FULL MOON (AQUARIUS) ANGELCODES: 6/11	4
	9	10	11
	16	17	18 NEW MOON (LEO) ANGELCODES: 3/8
	23	24	25
	30	31	

2020

WEDNESDAY	THURSDAY	FRIDAY	SATURDAY
			1
5	6	7	8
12	13	14	15
19	20	21	22
26	27	28	29

August Full Moon

DATE: MONDAY, AUGUST 3 / LUNATION: 11:59 AM (NEW YORK)
ASTRO SIGN: 11° AQUARIUS / RULERS: SATURN, URANUS
ELEMENT: AIR / EXPRESSION: FIXED
ARCHANGEL: GABRIEL

FULL MOON KEYWORDS: COMPLETION, SURRENDER

LUNA'S ASTRO ENERGIES

When Lady Luna is shining her Aquarian light, she's inviting you to tune in to your mind and the secret visions that you create. Aquarian light shines on your inner humanitarian, philanthropist and making the world a better place. As you prepare to surrender during this full moon Lady Luna is inviting you to surrender anything that keeps you from making the world a better place.

AUGUST 3 AQUARIUS FULL MOON ANGEL CODE 6/11

OVERLIGHTING ANGEL CODE 6 | GATEWAY OF INFINITE KNOWING
Activation: Activates your intuition in all realms and dimensions.

Darling Heart Spirit! You came to Earth to experience a life on the material plane, yet you are a very powerful intuitive! Intuitive knowing is one of your many gifts of spirit! This month, you're invited to reawaken your infinite knowing. The angels are reminding you that you are a magnificent Spirit Being experiencing a life in matter. You are one with the Universe and all can be known. Remember, Dear Heart, you are a Master Intuitive.

ARCHANGEL ARIEL'S MESSAGE 6 | GATEWAY OF INFINITE KNOWING

Dear One, remember you are a masterful intuitive being. You are not of the Earth, yet part of you is in your Earth Body. There is so much more. You are a masterful intuitive and as you awaken, you will tune into the infinite knowing … unexpected at first and then proceeding at will. Opening your God's Eye of Infinite Knowing connects you to the Whole of Life and the Whole of Your Being!

LUNATION ANGEL CODE 11 | GATEWAY TO THE GALAXIES
Activation: Activates your expansion of consciousness to travel beyond time and space.

This angel code invites you to expand your consciousness, surrender limitations, and journey beyond time and space. Angels invite you to understand clocks are an agreement made by society to keep things running smoothly in the everyday ... Angels invite you to play with time and space. Stay fully present in the moment in that place of no time and no space. Stay in the knowing that there is no time nor space beyond the present. Remember, the Sun is also activating 11!

ARCHANGEL ARIEL'S MESSAGE 11 | GATEWAY TO THE GALAXIES

And so, Dear One, here we have the activation of the Angel Code 11 | Gateway to the Galaxies. Sweet One, you are a limitless being. Your natural state of being knows no boundaries ... knows no clocks. There is limitless freedom as you allow yourself to experience your Galactic self! As was written in an earth song "We are Stardust" and so you are.

AUGUST 3 AQUARIUS FULL MOON ACTIVATION FOR VIBRANT HEALTH

Full Moons activate completion and surrendering things in your life that no longer serve a purpose. And, of course, Sweet One, always surrender with love and gratitude. You now have the powerful support of Archangel Gabriel and Lady Luna in her Aquarian energies. We are inviting you, this Full Moon, for the third time this year, to surrender habits and choices that block your Vibrant Health! And, of course, Dear One, Vibrant Health is more than physical well-being! It's your whole self ... mind ... body ... and soul!

Please take some quiet time this week feeling into the **Angel Codes 6 | Gateway Of Infinite Knowing and 11 | Gateway to the Galaxies**. Feel into **Lady Luna's Astro Energies of Uranus ruled Aquarius**. Here Luna flies through the Cosmos, socializing and chatting with everyone she sees... usually on her devices!! How can you use these energies to help you surrender blocks to VIBRANT HEALTH?

Darling Heart, we invite you to spend some quiet time on Monday tuning into your beautiful Infinite Heart, feeling into your dreams and wishes. Feeling into your Health. On this Full Moon decide on one thing you want to surrender that you believe is keeping you from experiencing your perfect Vibrant Health. To help you sort it out, call on Archangel Gabriel, Angel of Aquarius, Angel of Inspiration and Divine Communication. Here's our checklist:

On a scale of 1 – 10 what's your number? _____
(10 is absolutely perfect vibrant health, 1 is being treated for illness)

Darling Heart here are some things to consider:

How often are you moving your body? (yoga, tai chi, qigong, running, walking, gym exercise, etc.)
　　1x week____ 3x week____ more than 3x week_____ I'm inconsistent____ not at all _____

Are you eating foods to keep you vibrant? yes____ no__

Are you underweight? ____ overweight? _____

Do you meditate? 1x week____ 3x week__ more than 3x week__ I'm inconsistent__
not at all _

Are you sleeping well? yes ____ no __ sometimes _____

How much time do you spend on your screen/devices daily? minutes __ hours __

Are you balancing work and play/family/friends? yes __ no__

Are you leaking energy by holding on to anger, blame, disappointment or loss? yes__ no __

Are you holding on to guilt? yes __ no____

Look at what you've written and name one thing you are willing to surrender this Full Moon that you believe blocks your Vibrant Health.

_____

AUGUST 3 AQUARIUS FULL MOON FIRE CEREMONY OF SURRENDER

Gather Your Sacred Tools:

- The Angel Code Oracle 2020
- A candle and lighter
- A fireproof bowl
- A small piece of paper for burning
- A pen or pencil

Go to a space where you won't be disturbed. Call in Archangel Gabriel to help you come fully into your shining heart as you release with love and gratitude. Write whatever you are surrendering on a small slip of paper. Read what you've written out loud. You might use these words:

"By the light of this full moon I surrender _____to the Sacred Fires. I surrender with Love and Gratitude and I am now complete with _____."

Then light your paper and watch it burn. Knowing you have surrendered, released and are now complete. Sit for a moment. Feel into the power of surrender. And now write whatever impressions, feelings and awareness you have. _____

_____

_____

Thank Archangel Gabriel and Lady Luna and extinguish your fire.

What to do with the ashes? Many people choose to bury them. I like to go outside by the light of the moon, hold the ashes in my palm and blow them away!

Darling Heart, a surrendering ceremony is really powerful …trust that whatever you have released no longer has power over you and be sure not to re-invoke it into your life!

AUG

august

S	M	T	W	T	F	S
						1
2	3	4	5	6	7	8
9	10	11	12	13	14	15
16	17	18	19	20	21	22
23	24	25	26	27	28	29
30	31					

notes

3 MONDAY	**4** TUESDAY	**5** WEDNESDAY
FULL MOON ASTRO SIGN: AQUARIUS ANGELCODES: 6/11		

6 THURSDAY	**7** FRIDAY	**8** SATURDAY	**9** SUNDAY

AUG

august

S	M	T	W	T	F	S
						1
2	3	4	5	6	7	8
9	10	11	12	13	14	15
16	17	18	19	20	21	22
23	24	25	26	27	28	29
30	31					

notes

10 MONDAY	**11** TUESDAY	**12** WEDNESDAY

13 THURSDAY	14 FRIDAY	15 SATURDAY	16 SUNDAY

August New Moon

DATE: TUESDAY, AUGUST 18 / LUNATION: 10:42 PM (NEW YORK)
ASTRO SIGN: 26° LEO / RULER: SUN
ELEMENT: FIRE / EXPRESSION: FIXED
ARCHANGEL: URIEL

NEW MOON KEYWORDS: NEW BEGINNINGS, CREATION

LUNA'S ASTRO ENERGIES

When Lady Luna shines her light on Sun ruled Leo, she basks in her moonlight as it activates her passion for life! Lady Luna is firmly rooted in her warm-hearted generosity! This lioness knows how to be the benevolent Queen! Lady Luna is inviting you to ignite your passion, and your warm-hearted generosity as you create your dreams during this Luna Portal of Creation.

AUGUST 18 LEO NEW MOON ANGEL CODE 3/8

OVERLIGHTING ANGEL CODE 3 | GATEWAY OF THE ILLUMINATED SELF
Activation: Activates Self-Empowerment as your embodied Light merges with the Divine All.

This code empowers you as your embodied light merges with the Divine All.

ARCHANGEL ARIEL'S MESSAGE 3 | GATEWAY OF THE ILLUMINATED SELF

Dear One, this code merges your Illuminated Self with the Divine Mother. Here you are brought into direct connection to the Divine through the Divine Mother essence. As you feel into these frequencies, understand you are not alone. You came to Earth with a whole team guiding you. Not only angels, the ascended masters are here too. So, we invite you to call on the masters. There are many. Who resonates with you? Quan Yin? Yogananda? Yeshua/Jesus? Mary? There are many. You have lived many lifetimes and have related with your guides through eons. And Dear One, there is no right or wrong. Call on those connected to your SoulHeart.

LUNATION ANGEL CODE 8 | GATEWAY OF INFINITE POSSIBILITIES
Activation: Activates your limitless possibilities. Life on Earth is meant to be lived with infinite abundance!

This code is an Infinity Code connecting you to your Infinite Soul, nourishing and replenishing you with the Light of Infinite Possibilities. When this light flows through you, you can access your Soul Experiences. The Sun is also activating 8!

ARCHANGEL ARIEL'S MESSAGE 8 | GATEWAY OF INFINITE POSSIBILITIES

You, Dear One, are a Divine Being holding the light of infinite possibilities. When you chose to incarnate on planet Earth you chose to experience all the delights this magical blue planet has to offer... creating an abundant, joyful, vibrantly healthy, loving life for yourself! As a cosmic soul you were aware only of limitless infinite possibility. We invite you to return to that knowing ... there are no limits and your life is truly filled with infinite possibilities awaiting you to choose the ones to activate!

AUGUST 18 LEO NEW MOON ACTIVATION FOR VIBRANT HEALTH

New Moon activates new beginnings, visioning, setting goals and creating while you have the powerful support of Archangel Uriel and Lady Luna. As we move through the Wheel of the Year, this New Moon is the third time we are inviting you to uplevel your VIBRANT HEALTH! This time though the fiery energies of Leo!! And, of course, Sweet One, VIBRANT HEALTH is more than physical well-being! It's your whole self ... mind ... body ... and soul!

Please take some quiet time this week feeling into the **Angel Codes 3 | Gateway Of The Illuminated Self** and **8 | Gateway Of Infinite Possibilities.** Feel into **Lady Luna's Astro Energies of Sun ruled Leo.** Here Luna lights her fires of action! You've heard the expression "Put a fire under it!" How will you use these energies to help you light your fire and activate more VIBRANT HEALTH?

Darling Heart, we invite you to spend some quiet time on Tuesday tuning into your beautiful Infinite Heart, feeling into your dreams and wishes around your Health. Call on Archangel Uriel, Angel of Leo, Angel of Light and Clarity to help you clarify the change you are making as you create more VIBRANT HEALTH!

Sweet One, ask yourself the following question:

On a scale of 1 – 10 what's your number? _____
(10 is absolutely perfect vibrant health, 1 is being treated for illness)

And now, come to stillness and feel into your relationship with Your Health. Here are some common questions associated with Health. Check those that apply:

How often are you moving your body? (yoga, tai chi, qigong, running, walking, gym exercise, etc)
    1x week____ 3x week____ more than 3x week__ I'm inconsistent____ not at all ____

Are you eating foods to keep you vibrant? yes _____ no_____

Are you underweight? _____ overweight?_____

Do you meditate? 1x week_____ 3x week___ more than 3x week___ I'm inconsistent___ not at all ___

Are you sleeping well? yes _____ no ___ sometimes _____

How much time do you spend on your screen/devices daily? minutes _____ hours _____

Are you balancing work and play/family/friends? yes _____ no_____

Are you leaking energy by holding on to anger, blame, disappointment or loss? yes ___ no _____

Are you holding on to guilt? yes _____ no ____

From the questions above write down 3 possibilities you can create even more delicious VIBRANT HEALTH.

_____

_____

_____

Read each possibility out loud. Feel into them. Does one stand out from the other two? Does one bring a smile as you read it? Is one easier to manifest? Or do you feel the timing is right… Or not?

Which possibility on your list of 3 is the one to activate during this lunar cycle?

_____

AUGUST 18 LEO NEW MOON CEREMONY OF CREATION

Gather Your Sacred Tools:

- A candle and lighter
- Paper, pens, markers etc.
- The Angel Code Oracle 2020
- A pen or pencil

Sweet One, go to a space where you won't be disturbed and light your candle. Call in Archangel Uriel to help inspire you as you come fully into your shining heart preparing to activate your New Moon dream! Allow yourself plenty of time to play with this!

Review the possibility you decided to activate during this lunar cycle and write a creation statement (an intention) to activate more VIBRANT HEALTH. Remember your statement is to be in the present and not in the future!

_____

OK, Dear Heart, now let's turn that intention into a goal with 3 actionable steps!

3 actions I am taking in the next two weeks to manifest more VIBRANT HEALTH!

_____

_____

_____

Awesome! You now have a goal and 3 actionable steps to take!

Here's the next part of your New Moon Creation Ceremony! We invite you to create a mini angel board! It's a vision board with the Angels! On your paper using your pens and markers write your intention and the 3 actions you are taking in the next two weeks!

Be sure to write Thank You on your board. You can write a simple Thank You or something more elaborate, "Thank You Angels and Lady Luna for this and all deliciousness I'm creating now!"

Be creative! Create something you'd like to look at least once a day, each and EVERY day! Make it fun … catchy … playful!!

When you've completed your mini Angel Board put your tools away.

Thank Archangel Uriel and Lady Luna and extinguish your candle.

Be sure to place your Angel Board where you will see it every day for the next two weeks!

Here are some things you might like to do to keep your mini angel board in your awareness:

- Take a picture on your phone and make it your screen saver.
- Take a photo on your computer and make it your screen saver.
- Frame it and put it on your desk or in your kitchen.
- Keep it on your bed stand. It's great seeing it first thing in the morning and again just before falling asleep!

Dear Heart, FOLLOW YOUR ACTIONABLE STEPS! When you DO something toward your goals you are actually creating an energetic alignment. And you know alignment helps you manifest more quickly!

AUG

august

S M T W T F S
            1
2 3 4 5 6 7 8
9 10 11 12 13 14 15
16 17 18 19 20 21 22
23 24 25 26 27 28 29
30 31

notes

17 MONDAY	**18** TUESDAY	**19** WEDNESDAY
	NEW MOON ASTRO SIGN: LEO QANGELCODES: 3/8	

20 THURSDAY	**21** FRIDAY	**22** SATURDAY	**23** SUNDAY

AUG
august

S	M	T	W	T	F	S
						1
2	3	4	5	6	7	8
9	10	11	12	13	14	15
16	17	18	19	20	21	22
23	24	25	26	27	28	29
30	31					

notes

24 MONDAY	25 TUESDAY	26 WEDNESDAY

27 THURSDAY	28 FRIDAY	29 SATURDAY	30 SUNDAY

September 2020 Overlighting Angel Code 4 | Gateway to The Infinite Heart

Activation: Activating your Light of Infinite Love shining through your Infinite SoulHeart.

September brings us the Overlighting Angel Code of 4 | GATEWAY TO THE INFINITE HEART. Darling Heart, you are a Cosmic Being of Infinite Heart. You came to Earth to experience a material life lived through your Divine SoulHeart. And this month this energetic signature is again greatly amplified because the Overlighting Angel Code for 2020 is also 4 Gateway to the Infinite Heart!

ARCHANGEL ARIEL'S MESSAGE 4 | GATEWAY TO THE INFINITE HEART

Remember Dear One, you are a Divine Being choosing a life in the physical form. It is your Infinite Heart that is meant to guide you … for you are meant to live on your planet as a Divine Being experiencing the most delicious life you can imagine. Only a portion of your Divine Being is within your physical form. You have many waiting to serve you … Angels, Guides, Ascended Masters, Cosmic Beings … Your connection to all of your Soul Gifts and talents is through your magnificent heart. Let your heart be your guide. When things resonate harmoniously move in that direction. When you are feeling discord, retreat. Allow your awareness of your SoulHeart frequencies to grow. When you are not sure, feel into your precious SoulHeart. Ask questions. Feel into your Heart. You will become more skilled as you practice!

SEPTEMBER ANGEL MANTRA

🦋 *"My Heart is my Inner Guidance System. The more I am aware of messages my Heart is sending and follow what feels good the more love, happiness and Joy I receive!"*

THIS MONTH'S ANGEL MANTRA ACTIVATION

Each morning, look into a mirror, begin taking long, slow, deep breaths all the way into your belly. As you breathe bring your awareness into your SoulHeart. Feel your beautiful SoulHeart expanding. Feel the shift.

Do you feel warm… or cool? Do you feel vibration? See color? Now, bring your awareness back to your breath and take 3 long, slow, deep breaths. On each outbreath, repeat or tone the Angel Mantra out loud:

🕊 *"My Heart is my Inner Guidance System. The more I am aware of messages my Heart is sending and follow what feels good the more love, happiness and Joy I receive!"*

Repeat for a total of 3 breaths. For an even deeper alignment, repeat this in the evenings, too!

Yoo-hoo! Angel Code Oracle 2021 is in production...

We're pleased to announce THE ANGEL CODE ORACLE 2021 is in production! Have you signed up for the waitlist, yet? It's easy. Just send an e-mail to:
Taco2021waitlist@katebeloved.com

We'll send an e-mail as soon as it's available!

We know you're creating an amazing year!
Abundant Angel Blessings
Beloveds

---

september

SUNDAY	MONDAY	TUESDAY
		1
6	7	8
13	14	15
20	21	22 EQUINOX
27	28	29

This Month

_____

_____

_____

_____

_____

_____

_____

_____

_____

_____

_____

_____

_____

2020

WEDNESDAY	THURSDAY	FRIDAY	SATURDAY
2 FULL MOON (PISCES) ANGEL CODES: 6/10	3	4	5
9	10	11	12
16	17 NEW MOON (VIRGO) ANGEL CODES: 3/7	18	19
23	24	25	26
30			

September Full Moon

DAY: WEDNESDAY, SEPTEMBER 2 / LUNATION: 1:23 AM (NEW YORK)
ASTRO SIGN: 10° PISCES / RULERS: JUPITER, NEPTUNE
ELEMENT: WATER / EXPRESSION: MUTABLE
ARCHANGEL: RAPHAEL

FULL MOON KEYWORDS: COMPLETION, SURRENDER

LUNA'S ASTRO ENERGIES

When Lady Luna comes to her fullness in her shining Piscean light, she aligns with deep intuition. Although, like Mermaid Pisces, you may be swimming in your own rhythm, Lady Luna invites you not to get lost in your own watery paradise but to step into the wisdom of your intuition and create your dreams from that place of Inner Knowing. When you find darkness, shine your powerful non-judgmental, forgiving compassion into the darkness.

SEPTEMBER 2 PISCES FULL MOON ANGEL CODE 6/10

OVERLIGHTING ANGEL CODE 6 | GATEWAY OF INFINITE KNOWING
Activation: Activates your intuition in all realms and dimensions.

Darling Heart Spirit! You came to earth to experience a life on the material plane, yet you are a very powerful intuitive! Intuitive knowing is one of your many gifts of spirit! This month, you're invited to reawaken your infinite knowing. The Angels are reminding you that you are a magnificent Spirit Being experiencing a life in matter. You are one with the Universe and all can be known. Remember, Dear Heart, you are a Master Intuitive.

ARCHANGEL ARIEL'S MESSAGE 6 | GATEWAY OF INFINITE KNOWING

Dear One, remember you are a masterful intuitive being. You are not of the Earth. Yet part of you is in your earth body… There is so much more. You are a masterful intuitive and as you awaken, you will tune into the infinite knowing… unexpected at first and then proceeding at will. Opening your God's Eye of Infinite Knowing connects you to the Whole of Life and the Whole of Your Being!

LUNATION ANGEL CODE 10 | GATEWAY OF THE UNIVERSAL LIGHT STAR
Activation: Activates Light unifying your physical Body Temple with your Light Body, Divine Light of the Universe and all Benevolent Light Beings.

The Angels are reminding you that you are a Light Being living in a physical human body. Here, they connect you to the Divine Light of the Universe and all Light Beings as they align your physical body with your Light Body. Do not hide your Light beneath the barrel… Shine Bright Dear One! Be sure to shine extra bright because the Sun is also activating 10!

ARCHANGEL ARIEL'S MESSAGE 10 | GATEWAY OF THE UNIVERSAL LIGHT STAR

Dear One, Angel Code 10 brings light from the universe into your physical body. Light holds the divine spark … light is energy. Energy of the universe is pouring through your physical Body Temple bringing spirit into matter… illuminating you with Divine Grace.

SEPTEMBER 2 PISCES FULL MOON ACTIVATION FOR MATERIAL WEALTH

Full Moon activates completion and surrendering things in your life that no longer serve you. And, of course Dear One, always surrender with love and gratitude. This Full Moon you have the powerful support of Archangel Raphael and Lady Luna in her Piscean energies as you're invited for the third time this year to surrender blocks to Material Wealth!

Please take some quiet time this week feeling into the **Angel Codes 6 | Gateway Of Infinite Knowing and 10 | Gateway Of The Universal Light Star**. Feel into **Lady Luna's Astro Energies of Neptune ruled Pisces**. Here Luna is in her deep watery soul energies. She longs to come into Oneness. How can you use these energies to help you surrender blocks to Material Wealth?

Darling Heart, we invite you to spend some quiet time on Wednesday tuning into your beautiful Infinite Heart, feeling into your dreams and wishes. Feeling into Wealth. On this Full Moon decide on one thing you want to surrender that you believe is keeping you from experiencing delicious Material Wealth. To help you sort it out, call on Archangel Raphael, Angel of Pisces, Angel of the Heart, Angel of Love, Healing and Forgiveness. Here's our checklist:

Material Wealth
On a scale of 1 – 10, what's your number? _____
(10 feeling absolutely divinely Wealthy, 1 wondering how you are going to pay your bills.)

Darling Heart, come to stillness and feel into your relationship with Money. Here are some common thoughts associated with money. Check those that apply.

How I Feel About My Money

I love having enough money to do all the things I love without ever having to think about
    how much it cost. _____

I just don't have enough for lot of extras. ____

I get a knot in my belly/ heart rate shifts when I think about money. __

Savings

I pay my savings account first. _____

I put money in my savings account every week/paycheck/month. _____

I have a retirement plan. ____

I don't have a solid plan. __

I live from paycheck to paycheck. ____

Purchases

I love new clothes and buy cute things when I see them. _____

I can afford the things I want (gym/classes/conferences/vacations/travel). __

I rarely buy anything new. _____

Credit Cards

I use my charge accounts and pay them off every month. _____

I use my charge accounts and carry a balance. _____

I use my charge cards and pay the minimum each month. ____

Look at what you've checked and name one thing you are willing to surrender this Full Moon that you believe blocks your Material Wealth.

_____

SEPTEMBER 2 PISCES FULL MOON FIRE CEREMONY OF SURRENDER

Gather Your Sacred Tools:

- ❦ The Angel Code Oracle 2020
- ❦ A candle and lighter
- ❦ A fireproof bowl
- ❦ A small piece of paper for burning
- ❦ A pen or pencil

Sweet One, go to a space where you won't be disturbed and light your candle. Call in Archangel Raphael to help you come fully into your shining heart as you release with love and gratitude. Write whatever you are surrendering on a small slip of paper. Read what you've written out loud. You might use these words:

"By the light of this full moon I surrender _____ to the Sacred Fires. I surrender with Love and Gratitude and I am now complete with _____."

Then light your paper and watch it burn. Knowing you have surrendered, released and are now complete. Sit for a moment. Feel into the power of surrender. And now write whatever impressions, feelings, awareness you have. _____
_____
_____
_____

Thank Archangel Raphael and Lady Luna and extinguish your fire.

What to do with the ashes? Many people choose to bury them. I like to go outside by the light of the moon, hold the ashes in my palm and blow them away!

Darling Heart, a surrendering ceremony is really powerful …trust that whatever you have released no longer has power over you and be sure not to re-invoke it into your life!

SEPT

september

S	M	T	W	T	F	S
		1	2	3	4	5
6	7	8	9	10	11	12
13	14	15	16	17	18	19
20	21	22	23	24	25	26
27	28	29	30			

notes

31 MONDAY	**1** TUESDAY	**2** WEDNESDAY
		FULL MOON ASTRO SIGN: PISCES ANGEL CODES: 6/10

3 THURSDAY	**4** FRIDAY	**5** SATURDAY	**6** SUNDAY

SEPT

september

S	M	T	W	T	F	S
		1	2	3	4	5
6	7	8	9	10	11	12
13	14	15	16	17	18	19
20	21	22	23	24	25	26
27	28	29	30			

notes

7 MONDAY	8 TUESDAY	9 WEDNESDAY

10 THURSDAY	11 FRIDAY	12 SATURDAY	13 SUNDAY

September New Moon

DATE: THURSDAY, SEPTEMBER 17 / LUNATION: 7:00 AM (NEW YORK)
ASTRO SIGN: 25° VIRGO / RULER: MERCURY
ELEMENT: EARTH / MUTABLE
ARCHANGEL: MICHAEL

NEW MOON KEYWORDS: NEW BEGINNINGS, CREATION

LUNA'S ASTRO ENERGIES

When Lady Luna is in her Mercury ruled Virgo energies, you can enjoy working hard, methodically organizing, analyzing everything and paying great attention to detail as you move your heart's desires from dreams into goals with easy- to- follow plans! Lady Luna is reminding you that when you align with these powerful Virgo energies, amplified BIG TIME in this lunation, you have all the gear you need to bring your dreams to Life!

SEPTEMBER 17 VIRGO NEW MOON ANGEL CODE 3/7

OVERLIGHTING ANGEL CODE 3 | GATEWAY OF THE ILLUMINATED SELF
Activation: Activates Self-Empowerment as your embodied Light merges with the Divine All.

Empowering self as your embodied light merges with the Divine All. The angels are reminding you that you are not alone.

ARCHANGEL ARIEL'S MESSAGE 3 | GATEWAY OF THE ILLUMINATED SELF

Dear One, this code merges your Illuminated Self with the Divine Mother. Here you are brought into direct connection with the Divine through the Divine Mother essence. As you feel into these frequencies, understand you are not alone. You came to earth with a whole team guiding you. Not only Angels, the ascended masters are here too. So, we invite you to call on the masters. Who resonates with you? Quan Yin? Yogananda? Yeshua/ Jesus? Mary? There are many. You have lived many lifetimes and have related with your guides through eons. And Dear One, there is no right or wrong. Call on those connected to your SoulHeart.

LUNATION ANGEL CODE 7 | GATEWAY TO THE DIVINE COLLECTIVE
Activation: Activates your connection to the Collective Consciousness.

Angel Code 7 activates the energetic signature of the Collective Consciousness! Here, you are reminded that you are a being of Divine Energy. You are part of the Divine Collective. Your thoughts and actions are energy forms that affect the whole of life … even the weather! This code is amplified because the Sun is also activating 7!

ARCHANGEL ARIEL'S MESSAGE 7 | GATEWAY TO THE DIVINE COLLECTIVE

Dear One, we invite you to awaken to the knowledge that All Are One. There is a collective … no separation. You are part of the Whole. What you do, what you say, and what you think affects the Whole of Life… not just beings who breathe but the mountains, seas, waters, weather. All are a reflection of the energetic signature sent forth. Do you believe the words you speak are just words? Or do you understand the power they hold? You are a powerful creator! Once you breathe life into your words by speaking them aloud you have set a powerful invocation. You have released the energetic signature of those words into the universe. And the energy will build as it gathers more energy that is in vibrational coherence with its energetic signatures. Dear One, by the words you speak you can create Peace, Love, Kindness and Happiness in the collective or you can create War, Destruction, Disease and Divisiveness. What you create affects the whole of humanity. Keep your thoughts uplifted. Treat others with respect. Care for your planet. Understand All Are One and YOU affect the Whole! Now that you hold this understanding, we know you will create from your Divine SoulHeart.

SEPTEMBER 17 VIRGO NEW MOON ACTIVATION FOR MATERIAL WEALTH

New Moon activates new beginnings, visioning, setting goals and creating while you have the powerful support of Archangel Michael and Lady Luna. On the last Full Moon, you were invited to surrender something that blocks your MATERIAL WEALTH so now, on this New Moon, we invite you for the third time to create more wealth in your life!

As we move through the Wheel of the Year, this New Moon is the third time we are inviting you to manifest MATERIAL WEALTH!

Please take some quiet time this week feeling into the **Angel Codes 3 | Gateway Of The Illuminated Self** and **7 | Gateway To The Divine Collective**. Feel into **Lady Luna's Astro Energies of Mercury ruled Virgo**. Here Luna in her earthiness is organized, methodical and detail oriented. How can you use these energies help you create more MATERIAL WEALTH?

Darling Heart, we invite you to spend some quiet time on Thursday tuning into your beautiful Infinite Heart, feeling into your dreams and wishes around your Material Wealth. Call on Archangel Michael Archangel of Virgo, Angel of Strength and Courage to bring you strength and courage to call your dream into reality as you manifest more MATERIAL WEALTH!

Sweet One, ask yourself the following question:

Material Wealth
On a scale of 1 – 10 what's your number? _____
(10 feeling absolutely divinely wealthy, 1 wondering how you are going to pay your bills)

And now, Sweet One, come to stillness and feel into your relationship with Money. Here are some common thoughts associated with money. Check those that apply:

How I Feel About My Money
I love having enough money to do all the things I love without ever having to think about how much
    it cost. _____
I just don't have enough lots of extras. ____
I get a knot in my belly/ heart rate shifts when I think about money. ____

Savings
I pay my savings account first. _____
I put money in my savings account every week/paycheck/month. _____
I have a retirement plan. ____
I don't have a solid plan. __
I live from paycheck to paycheck. ____

Purchases
I love new clothes and buy cute things when I see them. _____
I can afford the things I want (gym/classes/conferences/vacations/travel). __
I rarely buy anything new. _____

Credit Cards
I use my charge accounts and pay them off every month. _____
I use my charge accounts and carry a balance. _____
I use my charge cards and pay the minimum each month. ____

From the list above and write down 3 possible ways you can create even more MATERIAL WEALTH.

_____

_____

_____

Read each possibility out loud. Feel into them. Does one stand out from the other two? Does one bring a smile as you read it? Is one easier to manifest? Or do you feel the timing is right… Or not?

Which possibility on your list of 3 is the one to activate during this lunar cycle?

_____

SEPTEMBER 17 VIRGO NEW MOON CEREMONY OF CREATION

Gather Your Sacred Tools:

- The Angel Code Oracle 2020
- A candle and lighter
- Paper, pens, markers etc.
- A pen or pencil

Sweet One, go to a space where you won't be disturbed and light your candle. Call in Archangel Michael to help inspire you as you come fully into your shining heart preparing to activate your New Moon dream! Allow yourself plenty of time to play with this!

Review the possibility you decided to activate during this lunar cycle and write a creation statement (an intention) to activate more Material Wealth. Remember your statement is to be in the present and not in the future!

_____

OK, Dear Heart, now let's turn that intention into a goal with 3 actionable steps!

3 actions I am taking in the next two weeks to manifest more MATERIAL WEALTH!

_____

_____

_____

Awesome! You now have a goal and 3 actionable steps to take!

Here's the next part of your New Moon Creation Ceremony! We invite you to create a mini angel board! It's a vision board with the Angels! On your paper using your pens and markers write your intention and the 3 actions you are taking in the next two weeks!

Be sure to write Thank You on your board. You can write a simple Thank You or something more elaborate, "Thank You Angels and Lady Luna for this and all deliciousness I'm creating now!"

Be creative! Create something you'd like to look at least once a day, each and EVERY day! Make it fun … catchy … playful!!

When you've completed your mini angel board put your tools away.

Thank Archangel Michael and Lady Luna and extinguish your candle.

Be sure to place your Angel Board where you will see it every day for the next two weeks!

Here are some things you might like to do to keep your mini angel board in your awareness:

- Take a picture on your phone and make it your screen saver.
- Take a photo on your computer and make it your screen saver.
- Frame it and put it on your desk or in your kitchen.
- Keep it on your bed stand. It's great seeing it first thing in the morning and again just before falling asleep!

Dear Heart, FOLLOW YOUR ACTIONABLE STEPS! When you DO something toward your goals you are actually creating an energetic alignment. And you know alignment helps you manifest more quickly!

SEPT

september

S	M	T	W	T	F	S
		1	2	3	4	5
6	7	8	9	10	11	12
13	14	15	16	17	18	19
20	21	22	23	24	25	26
27	28	29	30			

notes

14
MONDAY

15
TUESDAY

16
WEDNESDAY

17 THURSDAY	**18** FRIDAY	**19** SATURDAY	**20** SUNDAY
NEW MOON ASTRO SIGN: VIRGO ANGEL CODES: 3/7			

SEPT

september

S	M	T	W	T	F	S
		1	2	3	4	5
6	7	8	9	10	11	12
13	14	15	16	17	18	19
20	21	22	23	24	25	26
27	28	29	30			

notes

21 MONDAY	**22** TUESDAY	**23** WEDNESDAY
	EQUINOX	

24 THURSDAY	25 FRIDAY	26 SATURDAY	27 SUNDAY

October 2020 Overlighting Angel Code 5 | Gateway to The Angelic Triangle

Activation: Activates your connection to direct angel communication through the Angelic Triangle.

* To activate The Angelic Triangle, place your thumbs on your throat and your fingers on your ears. Do you feel the Triangle? Be still. Is there a Truth you need to speak? Is there a message you need to hear?

How delicious! October brings us once again the overlighting energetic signature Angel Code 5, your connection to the Angelic Realm through the Angelic Triangle. The angels are reminding you to call on them. Invite them into your life. Darling Heart, each time an Angel Code is revisited you are invited to go deeper!

ARCHANGEL ARIEL'S MESSAGE 5 | GATEWAY TO THE ANGELIC TRIANGLE

Yes. As Little One has said, you are invited here to deepen your relationship with your angels. Nurture your relationship with your angels the way you nurture your relationship with your best friend. Do you call your best friend to chat or visit … sharing the happenings of your life … asking for advice or opinions when needed?

Would you miss your friend if time was long between visits? And yet when once again you meet, is it not as though no time has elapsed? Do you know each other so well that the passage of time makes no difference? And yet, Dear One, does it not make your life sweeter, more fragrant, more delicious to have long chats, share secrets and enjoy tea together? This is how it is with your angels. We are ever present, and your angels know you can get busy with life in the third dimension and sometimes you might forget to invite your angels. Dear One, life is so much sweeter and more fragrant when you have long chats, share secrets and enjoy life in the company of angels!

OCTOBER ANGEL MANTRA

- *"Angels are waiting for my invitation to join me as partners, playmates and guides. All I have to do is ask!"*

THIS MONTH'S ANGEL MANTRA ACTIVATION

Each morning, look into a mirror, begin taking long, slow, deep breaths all the way into your belly. As you breathe bring your awareness into your SoulHeart. Feel your beautiful SoulHeart expanding. Feel the shift. Do you feel warm… or cool? Do you feel vibration? See color? Now, bring your awareness back to your breath and take 3 long, slow, deep breaths. On each outbreath, repeat or tone the Angel Mantra out loud:

🕊 *"Angels are waiting for my invitation to join me as partners, playmates and guides. All I have to do is ask!"*

Repeat for a total of 3 breaths. For an even deeper alignment, repeat this in the evenings, too!

Yoo-hoo! Angel Code Oracle 2021 is in production…

We're pleased to announce THE ANGEL CODE ORACLE 2021 is in production! Have you signed up for the waitlist, yet? It's easy. Just send an e-mail to:
Taco2021waitlist@katebeloved.com

We'll send an e-mail as soon as it's available!

We know you're creating an amazing year!
Abundant Angel Blessings
Beloveds

---

october

SUNDAY	MONDAY	TUESDAY
4	5	6
11	12	13
18	19	20
25	26	27

2020

WEDNESDAY	THURSDAY	FRIDAY	SATURDAY
	1 FULL MOON (ARIES) ANGEL CODES: 6/9	2	3
7	8	9	10
14	15	16 NEW MOON (LIBRA) ANGEL CODES: 12/5 *MERCURY RETROGRADE*	17
21	22	23	24
28	29	30	31 FULL MOON (TAURUS)

October Full Moon

DATE: THURSDAY, OCTOBER 1 / LUNATION: 5:06 PM (NEW YORK)
ASTRO SIGN: 9° ARIES / RULER: MARS
ELEMENT: FIRE / EXPRESSION: CARDINAL
ARCHANGEL: URIEL

FULL MOON KEYWORDS: COMPLETION, SURRENDER

LUNA'S ASTRO ENERGIES

Lady Luna is shining her light through Mars ruled Aries stirring your passion and up-leveling your confidence. Can't you feel it? Are you motivated by wild enthusiasm and just can't wait to begin that new project, relationship or just something new? No? Time to surrender whatever you believe is holding you back!

OCTOBER 1 ARIES FULL MOON ANGEL CODE 6/9

OVERLIGHTING ANGEL CODE 6 | GATEWAY OF INFINITE KNOWING
Activation: Activates your intuition in all realms and dimensions.

Darling Heart Spirit! You came to earth to experience a life on the material plane, yet you are a very powerful intuitive! Intuitive knowing is one of your many gifts of spirit! The Angels are reminding you that you are a magnificent Spirit Being experiencing a life in matter. You are one with the Universe and all can be known. Remember, Dear Heart, you are a Master Intuitive.

ARCHANGEL ARIEL'S MESSAGE 6 | GATEWAY OF INFINITE KNOWING

Dear One, remember you are a masterful intuitive being. You are not of the Earth. Yes, part of your being is in your Earth Body…. Yet, there is so much more to you. You are a multi-dimensional cosmic being and as such you may know and understand many dimensions and unseen realms. You are a masterful Intuitive and as you awaken you will tune into the Infinite Knowing…. Through the Eye of God! Unexpected knowings at first and then skill to tune in when you are wanting information. Synchronicities are your validation of opening God's Eye of Infinite Knowing. The more synchronicities you notice in your life, the more you understand your God's Eye is indeed opening! Remember too, Dear One, you are one with the universe and all can be known!

LUNATION ANGEL CODE 9 | GATEWAY OF DIVINE BLESSINGS
Activation: Activates your soul gifts and communication with benevolent Cosmic Beings; Angels, Star Beings, and Unseen Guides.

This angel code is the energetic signature that awakens your soul gifts and opens your communications to all angels, star beings, and guides throughout the cosmos. The Sun is also activating 9 so blessings abound!!!

ARCHANGEL'S ARIELS MESSAGE 9 | GATEWAY OF DIVINE BLESSINGS

Dear One, you are a Divine Being of Spirit. We are reminding you that you are awakening to your Soul Gifts. You have many Soul Gifts; some are known to you and some are not. As you awaken your gifts you can communicate with Angels, Star Beings, and Guides throughout the Cosmos. These benevolent beings are here awaiting your invitation to join you on your Earth journey.

OCTOBER 1 ARIES FULL MOON ACTIVATION FOR LOVE

Full Moons activate completion and surrendering things in your life that no longer serve a purpose. And, of course, Sweet One, always surrender with love and gratitude. You now have the powerful support of Archangel Uriel and Lady Luna in her Aries energies. This Full Moon you are invited for the fourth time this year to surrender blocks to Love!

Please take some quiet time this week feeling into the **Angel Codes 6 | Gateway Of Infinite Knowing** and **9 | Gateway Of Divine Blessings**. Feel into **Lady Luna's Astro Energies of Mars ruled Aries**. Here Luna is in on Fire and ready to ignite your dreams!! How can you use these energies to help you surrender blocks to LOVE?

Darling Heart, we invite you to spend some quiet time on Thursday tuning into your beautiful Infinite Heart, feeling into your dreams and wishes. Feeling into Love. On this Full Moon, the third Full Moon opportunity to surrender blocks to Love, decide on one thing you want to surrender that you believe is keeping your Heart from experiencing its most delicious Joy. To help you sort it out, call on Archangel Uriel, Archangel of Aries, Angel of Light to bring you clarity as you choose what to surrender! Here are some things to consider:

What is your passion? _____

_____

How do you express your fiery passions? _____

What makes your heart sing? _____

_____

Are you in a meaningful relationship? yes__ no__
If you answered no what is keeping you from being in a meaningful relationship?

_____

Other _____

Bonus Question
How much do you love yourself? What's your number? _____
On a scale of 1-10 (10 is *Yes! I'm absolutely totally awesome!* 1 is *I'm a mess. Totally unworthy of love.*)

If you rated yourself less than 10, what is keeping you from absolutely adoring your totally awesome self?

_____

_____

Look at what you've written and name one thing you are willing to surrender that you believe blocks LOVE in your life.

_____

_____

OCTOBER 1 ARIES FULL MOON FIRE CEREMONY OF SURRENDER

Gather Your Sacred Tools:

- The Angel Code Oracle 2020
- A candle and lighter
- A fireproof bowl
- A small piece of paper for burning
- A pen or pencil

Go to a space where you won't be disturbed and light your candle. Call in Archangel Uriel to help you come fully into your shining heart as you release with love and gratitude. Write whatever you are surrendering on a small slip of paper. Read what you've written out loud. You might use these words.

"By the light of this full moon I surrender _____to the Sacred Fires.
I surrender with Love and Gratitude and I am now complete with _____."

Then light your paper and watch it burn. Knowing you have surrendered, released and are now complete. Sit for a moment. Feel into the power of surrender. And now write whatever impressions, feelings and awareness you have.

_____

_____

_____

Thank Archangel Uriel and Lady Luna.

What to do with the ashes? Many people choose to bury them. I like to go outside by the light of the moon, hold the ashes in my palm and blow them away!

Darling Heart, a surrendering ceremony is really powerful…trust that whatever you have released no longer has power over you and be sure not to re-invoke it into your life!

OCT

october

S	M	T	W	T	F	S
				1	2	3
4	5	6	7	8	9	10
11	12	13	14	15	16	17
18	19	20	21	22	23	24
25	26	27	28	29	30	31

notes

28 MONDAY	29 TUESDAY	30 WEDNESDAY

1 THURSDAY	**2** FRIDAY	**3** SATURDAY	**4** SUNDAY
FULL MOON ASTRO SIGN: ARIES ANGEL CODES: 6/9			

OCT

october

S	M	T	W	T	F	S
				1	2	3
4	5	6	7	8	9	10
11	12	13	14	15	16	17
18	19	20	21	22	23	24
25	26	27	28	29	30	31

notes

5 MONDAY	**6** TUESDAY	**7** WEDNESDAY

8 THURSDAY	**9** FRIDAY	**10** SATURDAY	**11** SUNDAY

October New Moon

DATE: FRIDAY, OCTOBER 16 / LUNATION: 3:32 PM (NEW YORK)
ASTRO SIGN: 23° LIBRA / RULER: VENUS
ELEMENT: AIR / EXPRESSION: CARDINAL
ARCHANGEL: GABRIEL

NEW MOON KEYWORDS: NEW BEGINNINGS, CREATION

LUNA'S ASTRO ENERGIES

Darling Heart, during this new moon portal Lady Luna is inviting you to feel into her Libra energies. When she is in her Libra flow, she is cooperative, gracious, balanced and the queen of the ball! During this lunation, Luna reminds you to honor your flow as you create yumminess that aligns with your own natural rhythms!

OCTOBER 16 LIBRA NEW MOON ANGEL CODE 12/5

OVERLIGHTING ANGEL CODE 12 | GATEWAY TO THE HEART OF THE DIVINE MOTHER
Activation: Activates direct connection to the Divine through the Divine Mother Essence.

This Angel Code activates direct connection to the divine through the Divine Mother essence.

ARCHANGEL ARIEL'S MESSAGE 12 | GATEWAY TO THE HEART OF THE DIVINE MOTHER

Here we have the energetic signature of the Divine Mother... the essence of divinity of The All... of God, Goddess, Creator, Source, however you understand THE ONE. Understand this energy not as a mother you have known in physical form, but as a Divine Mother who comes in with the energetic signature of the Divine Creator and invites you to be open to the qualities of the Divine Feminine ... to understand that your world must now live through the SoulHeart. To live the qualities of the empowered mother... of divine feminine .... Those qualities of unconditional love ... of honoring ... cooperation ... respect ... and allowing others to be what they are meant to be ... to live their lives following their own paths ... and to live your earth journey in your way ... knowing that you are a multidimensional Divine Spiritual Being. Through the frequencies of the Divine Mother essence you are also connected to all essences of the divine ... you are one with Divine Energy.

LUNATION ANGEL CODE 5 | GATEWAY TO THE ANGELIC TRIANGLE
Activation: Activates your connection to direct angel communication through the Angelic Triangle * To activate The Angelic Triangle, place your thumbs on your throat and your fingers

on your ears. Do you feel the Triangle? Be still. Is there a Truth you need to speak? Is there a message you need to hear?

Darling Heart, the angels are reminding you to call on them. They are here for you so invite them into your life! And the Sun is also activating the 5!

ARCHANGEL ARIEL'S MESSAGE 5 | GATEWAY TO THE ANGELIC TRIANGLE

Dear One, you are always connected to the Angelic Realm. You came into this life with a council including many guides, teachers and angels. Your angels cannot participate in your life without an invitation. Ask your angels to play with you … to partner with you … to offer guidance. Just as we do here with Little One, whom you know as Beloved. Each morning when you arise invite your angels to play with you!

OCTOBER 16 LIBRA NEW MOON ACTIVATION FOR LOVE

New Moon activates new beginnings, visioning, setting goals and creating while you have the powerful support of Archangel Gabriel and Lady Luna. As we move through the Wheel of the Year, this New Moon is the fourth New Moon inviting you to focus on manifesting more LOVE in your life!

Please take some quiet time this week feeling into the **Angel Codes 12 | Gateway To The Heart Of The Divine Mother** and **5 | Gateway To The Angelic Triangle**. Feel into the **Lady Luna's Astro Energies of Venus ruled Libra**. Here airy Luna is flying through the Cosmos chatting with everyone she meets. She creates through communication. She creates balance, beauty and love! How can these energies help you activate more LOVE?

Darling Heart, we invite you to spend some quiet time on Friday tuning into your beautiful Infinite Heart, feeling into your dreams and wishes. Feeling in to Love. Call on Archangel Gabriel, Angel of Libra, Angel of Inspiration and Divine Communication to partner with you as you tune in to expressions of LOVE!

And now, Sweet One, ask yourself the following questions:

What is your passion? _____
_____

What makes your heart sing? _____
_____

What are your favorite ways of expressing romantic love in your life?
    writing__ art__ talking __ singing __ dancing _ touching __ eye gazing__ sex__
    other_____

What are your favorite ways of expressing non-romantic love in your life?

writing___ art___ talking ___ singing ___ dancing _ touching ___ eye gazing___
other_____

How can you bring more of that into your life during this Lunar cycle?

_____
_____
_____

From the questions above write down 3 dreams you'd like to create to bring more LOVE into your life.

_____
_____
_____

Read each dream out loud. Feel into them. Does one stand out from the other two? Does one bring a smile as you read it? Is one easier to manifest? Or do you feel the timing is right... Or not?

Which dream on your list of 3 is the one to activate during this lunar cycle?

_____

OCTOBER 16 LIBRA NEW MOON CEREMONY OF CREATION

Gather Your Sacred Tools:

- The Angel Code Oracle 2020
- A candle and lighter
- Paper, pens, markers etc.
- A pen or pencil

Sweet One, go to a space where you won't be disturbed and light your candle. Call in Archangel Gabriel to help inspire you as you come fully into your shining heart preparing to activate your New Moon dream! Allow yourself plenty of time to play with this!

Review the dream you decided to activate during this lunar cycle and write a creation statement (an intention) to create more LOVE in your life. Remember your statement is to be in the present and not in the future!

_____
_____

OK, Dear Heart, now let's turn that intention into a goal with 3 actionable steps!

3 actions I am taking in the next two weeks to manifest my intention to bring more delicious LOVE in my life!

_____

_____

_____

Awesome! You now have a goal and 3 actionable steps to take!

Here's the next part of your New Moon Creation Ceremony! We invite you to create a mini angel board! It's a vision board with the Angels! On your paper using your pens and markers write your intention and the 3 actions you are taking in the next two weeks!

Be sure to write Thank You on your board. You can write a simple Thank You or something more elaborate, "Thank You Angels and Lady Luna for this and all deliciousness I'm creating now!"

Be creative! Create something you'd like to look at least once a day, each and EVERY day! Make it fun … catchy … playful!!

When you've completed your mini angel board put your tools away.

Thank Archangel Gabriel and Lady Luna and extinguish your candle.

Be sure to place your Angel Board where you will see it every day for the next two weeks!

Here are some things you might like to do to keep your mini angel board in your awareness:

- Take a picture on your phone and make it your screen saver.
- Take a photo on your computer and make it your screen saver.
- Frame it and put it on your desk or in your kitchen.
- Keep it on your bed stand. It's great seeing it first thing in the morning and again just before falling asleep!

Dear Heart, FOLLOW YOUR ACTIONABLE STEPS! When you DO something toward your goals you are actually creating an energetic alignment. And you know alignment helps you manifest more quickly!

OCT

october

S	M	T	W	T	F	S
				1	2	3
4	5	6	7	8	9	10
11	12	13	14	15	16	17
18	19	20	21	22	23	24
25	26	27	28	29	30	31

notes

12 MONDAY	**13** TUESDAY	**14** WEDNESDAY

15 THURSDAY	**16** FRIDAY	**17** SATURDAY	**18** SUNDAY
	NEW MOON ASTRO SIGN: LIBRA ANGEL CODES: 12/5 *MERCURY RETROGRADE*		

OCT

october

S	M	T	W	T	F	S
				1	2	3
4	5	6	7	8	9	10
11	12	13	14	15	16	17
18	19	20	21	22	23	24
25	26	27	28	29	30	31

notes

19
MONDAY

20
TUESDAY

21
WEDNESDAY

22 THURSDAY	**23** FRIDAY	**24** SATURDAY	**25** SUNDAY

October Full Moon (Blue Moon)

DATE: SATURDAY, OCTOBER 31 / LUNATION: 10:51 AM (NEW YORK)
ASTRO SIGN: 8° TAURUS / RULER: VENUS
ELEMENT: EARTH / EXPRESSION: FIXED
ARCHANGEL: MICHAEL

FULL MOON KEYWORDS: COMPLETION, SURRENDER

LUNA'S ASTRO ENERGIES

When Lady Luna is in Venus ruled Taurus, she loves to be surrounded by love, luxury, beauty and material delights! During this Full Moon, Lady Luna invites you to look at your surroundings, your environment, your home. What doesn't belong? What are you holding onto that doesn't evoke beauty? Time to surrender! Remember Darling Heart, bring in only things you love!

OCTOBER 31 TAURUS FULL MOON ANGEL CODE 9/8

OVERLIGHTING ANGEL CODE 9 | GATEWAY OF DIVINE BLESSINGS
Activation: Activates your soul gifts and communication with benevolent Cosmic Beings; Angels, Star Beings, and Unseen Guides.

The Blessings of the Divine Angel Code is the energetic signature that activates your soul gifts and opens your communications to all angels, star beings and guides throughout the cosmos.

ARCHANGEL ARIEL'S MESSAGE 9 | GATEWAY OF DIVINE BLESSINGS

Dear One, you are a Divine Being of Spirit. We are reminding you that you are Awakening to your Soul Gifts. You have many Soul Gifts; some are known to you and some are not. As you awaken your gifts you can communicate with Angels, Star Beings and Guides throughout the Cosmos. These benevolent beings are here awaiting your invitation to join you on your Earth journey.

LUNATION ANGEL CODE 8 | GATEWAY OF INFINITE POSSIBILITIES
Activation: Activates your limitless possibilities. Life on Earth is meant to be lived with infinite abundance!

This code is an Infinity Code connecting you to your Infinite Soul, nourishing and replenishing you with the Light of Infinite Possibilities. Remember, the Sun also activates this 8!

ARCHANGEL ARIEL'S MESSAGE 8 | GATEWAY OF INFINITE POSSIBILITIES

You are an Infinite Being. Like the zero point, you have no beginning and no end. Remember, Dear One, your life has Infinite potential and Infinite possibilities. It is you who bring them into the Finite… who impose limitations on your Self. You have as much Infinite Potential today as the day you birthed onto this beautiful blue planet!

OCTOBER 31 TAURUS FULL MOON ACTIVATION FOR VIBRANT HEALTH

Full Moons activate completion and surrendering things in your life that no longer serve a purpose. And, of course, Sweet One, always surrender with love and gratitude. This Full Moon you have the powerful support of Archangel Michael and Lady Luna in her Taurean energies. This 2nd Full Moon of October you are invited for the fourth and final time this year to surrender blocks to Vibrant Health! And, of course, Dear One, Vibrant Health is more than physical well-being! It's your whole self … mind … body … and soul!

Please take some quiet time this week feeling into the **Angel Codes 9 | Gateway of Divine Blessings** and **8 | Gateway Of Infinite Possibilities**. Feel into **Lady Luna's Astro Energies of Venus ruled Taurus**. Here Luna is grounded by love and beauty she is so very patient! How can you use these energies to help you surrender blocks to your VIBRANT HEALTH?

Darling Heart, we invite you to spend some quiet time on Saturday tuning into your beautiful Infinite Heart, feeling into your dreams and wishes. Feeling into your Health. On this Full Moon decide on one thing you want to surrender that you believe is keeping you from experiencing your perfect Vibrant Health! To help you sort it out, call on Archangel Michael, Angel of Taurus, Angel of Strength and Courage. Step into your courageous strength and see where you can surrender blocks to your perfect Vibrant Health. Here's our checklist:

On a scale of 1 – 10, 1hat's your number? _____
(10 is absolutely perfect vibrant health, 1 is being treated for illness)

Darling Heart here are some things to consider:

How often are you moving your body? (yoga, tai chi, qigong, running, walking, gym exercise, etc)
    1x week____ 3x week_____ more than 3x week_____
I'm inconsistent____ Not at all _____

Are you eating foods to keep you vibrant? yes___ no___
Are you underweight? ___ overweight? _____
Do you meditate? 1x week___ 3x week__ more than 3x week__ I'm inconsistent__ not at all __
Are you sleeping well? Yes ___ No __ Sometimes _____
How much time do you spend on your screen/devices daily? minutes_____ hours__
Are you balancing work and play/family/friends? yes_____ no__
Are you leaking energy by holding on to anger, blame, disappointment or loss? yes__ no__
Are you holding on to guilt? yes___ no__

Look at what you've written and name one thing you are willing to surrender this Full Moon that you believe blocks your VIBRANT HEALTH.

_____

OCTOBER 31 TAURUS FULL MOON FIRE CEREMONY OF SURRENDER

Gather Your Sacred Tools:

- The Angel Code Oracle 2020
- A candle and lighter
- A fireproof bowl
- A small piece of paper for burning
- A pen or pencil

Go to a space where you won't be disturbed and light your candle. Call in Archangel Michael to help you come fully into your shining heart as you release with love and gratitude. Write whatever you are surrendering on a small slip of paper. Read what you've written out loud. You might use these words:

"By the light of this full moon I surrender _____to the Sacred Fires. I surrender with Love and Gratitude and I am now complete with _____."

Then light your paper and watch it burn. Knowing you have surrendered, released and are now complete. Sit for a moment. Feel into the power of surrender. And now write whatever impressions, feelings and awareness you have. _____

_____
_____
_____

Thank Archangel Michael and Lady Luna and extinguish your fire.

What to do with the ashes? Many people choose to bury them. I like to go outside by the light of the moon, hold the ashes in my palm and blow them away!

Darling Heart, a surrendering ceremony is really powerful … trust that whatever you have released no longer has power over you and be sure not to re-invoke it into your life!

OCT

october

S	M	T	W	T	F	S
				1	2	3
4	5	6	7	8	9	10
11	12	13	14	15	16	17
18	19	20	21	22	23	24
25	26	27	28	29	30	31

notes

26 MONDAY	27 TUESDAY	28 WEDNESDAY

29 THURSDAY	30 FRIDAY	31 SATURDAY	1 SUNDAY
		FULL MOON *BLUE MOON* ASTRO SIGN: TAURUS ANGEL CODES: 9/8	

November 2020 Overlighting Angel Code
6 | Gateway of Infinite Knowing

Activation: Activates your intuition in all realms and dimensions.

The Overlighting Angel Code for this month is 6 | GATEWAY OF INFINITE KNOWING. Darling Heart Spirit! You came to Earth to experience a life on the material plane, yet you are a very powerful intuitive! Intuitive knowing is one of your many gifts of spirit! This month, you're invited to reawaken your infinite knowing. The angels are reminding you that you are a magnificent Spirit Being experiencing a life in matter. You are one with the Universe and all can be known. Remember, Dear Heart, you are a Master Intuitive.

ARCHANGEL ARIEL'S MESSAGE 6 | GATEWAY OF INFIINITE KNOWING

Dear One, remember you are a masterful intuitive being. You are not of the Earth. Yes, part of your being is in your Earth Body …. Yet, there is so much more to you. You are a multi- dimensional cosmic being and as such you may know and understand many dimensions and unseen realms You are a masterful Intuitive and as you awaken you will tune into the Infinite Knowing …. Through the Eye of God! ... Unexpected knowings at first and then skill to tune in when you are wanting information. Synchronicities are your validation of opening God's Eye of Infinite Knowing. The more synchronicities you notice in your life, the more you understand your God's Eye is indeed opening! Remember too, Dear One, you are one with the universe and all can be known!

NOVEMBER ANGEL MANTRA

> ❦ *"I am a being of Infinite Knowing. The more I follow my intuition the more accurate I become!"*

THIS MONTH'S ANGEL MANTRA ACTIVATION

Each morning, look into a mirror, begin taking long, slow, deep breaths all the way into your belly. As you breathe bring your awareness into your SoulHeart. Feel your beautiful SoulHeart expanding. Feel the shift. Do you feel warm… or cool? Do you feel vibration? See color? Now, bring your awareness back to your breath and take 3 long, slow, deep breaths. On each outbreath, repeat or tone the Angel Mantra out loud:

🕊 *"I am a being of Infinite Knowing. The more I follow my intuition the more accurate I become!"*

Repeat for a total of 3 breaths. For an even deeper alignment, repeat this in the evenings, too!

november

This Month

SUNDAY	MONDAY	TUESDAY
1	2 MERCURY DIRECT	3
8	9	10
15 NEW MOON (SCORPIO) ANGEL CODES: 12/5	16	17
22	23	24
29	30 FULL MOON ECLIPSE (GEMINI) ANGEL CODES: 9/8	

2020

WEDNESDAY	THURSDAY	FRIDAY	SATURDAY
4	5	6	7
11	12	13	14
18	19	20	21
25	26	27	28

NOV

november

S	M	T	W	T	F	S
1	2	3	4	5	6	7
8	9	10	11	12	13	14
15	16	17	18	19	20	21
22	23	24	25	26	27	28
29	30					

notes

2 MONDAY	**3** TUESDAY	**4** WEDNESDAY
MERCURY DIRECT		

5 THURSDAY	6 FRIDAY	7 SATURDAY	8 SUNDAY

November New Moon

DATE: SUNDAY NOVEMBER 15 / LUNATION: 12:08 AM (NEW YORK)
ASTRO SIGNS: 23° SCORPIO / RULERS: MARS, PLUTO
ELEMENT: WATER / EXPRESSION: FIXED
ARCHANGEL: RAPHAEL

NEW MOON KEYWORDS: NEW BEGINNINGS, CREATION

LUNA'S ASTRO ENERGIES

Lady Luna is activating Pluto/Mars ruled Scorpio. Passions run hot. Lady Luna in Watery Scorpio shines her light on your deep emotions. In this Lunar Portal of Creation accept Lady Luna's invitation to create magic in the very deepest part of your soul!

NOVEMBER 15 SCORPIO NEW MOON ANGEL CODE 12/5

OVERLIGHTING ANGEL CODE 12 | GATEWAY TO THE HEART OF THE DIVINE MOTHER
Activation: Activates direct connection to the Divine through the Divine Mother Essence.

This Angel code activates direct connection to the divine through the Divine Mother essence.

ARCHANGEL ARIEL'S MESSAGE 12 | GATEWAY TO THE HEART OF THE DIVINE MOTHER

Here we have the energetic signature of the Divine Mother … the essence of divinity of The All … of God, Goddess, Creator, Source, however you understand THE ONE. Understand this energy not as a mother you have known in physical form, but as a Divine Mother who comes in with the energetic signature of the Divine Creator and invites you to be open to the qualities of the Divine Feminine … to understand that your world must now live through the SoulHeart. To live the qualities of the empowered mother … of divine feminine …. Those qualities of unconditional love … of honoring … cooperation … respect … and allowing others to be what they are meant to be … to live their lives following their own paths … and to live your earth journey in your way … knowing that you are a multidimensional Divine Spiritual Being. Through the frequencies of the Divine Mother essence you are also connected to all essences of the divine … you are one with Divine Energy.

LUNATION ANGEL CODE 5 | GATEWAY TO THE ANGELIC TRIANGLE

Activation: Activates your connection to direct angel communication through the Angelic Triangle. * To activate The Angelic Triangle, place your thumbs on your throat and your fingers on your ears. Do you feel the Triangle? Be still. Is there a Truth you need to speak? Is there a message you need to hear?

Darling Heart, the angels are reminding you to call on them. They are there for you so invite them into your life! This code is amplified as the Sun is also activating the 5!

ARCHANGEL ARIEL'S MESSAGE 5 | GATEWAY TO THE ANGELIC TRIANGLE

Dear One, you are always connected to the Angelic Realm. You came into this life with a council including many guides, teachers and angels. Your angels cannot participate in your life without an invitation. Ask your angels to play with you … to partner with you … to offer guidance. Just as we do here with Little One, who you know as Beloved. Each morning when you arise invite your angels to play with you!

NOVEMBER 15 SCORPIO NEW MOON ACTIVATION FOR VIBRANT HEALTH

New Moon activates new beginnings, visioning, setting goals and creating while you have the powerful support of Archangel Raphael and Lady Luna. As we move through the Wheel of the Year, this New Moon is the fourth time and final time we are inviting you to uplevel your VIBRANT HEALTH in 2020! And, of course, Sweet One, VIBRANT HEALTH is more than physical well-being! It's your whole self … mind … body … and soul!

Please take some quiet time this week feeling into the **Angel Codes 12 | Gateway To The Heart of The Divine Mother** and **5 | Gateway To The Angelic Triangle**. Feel into the **Lady Luna's Astro Energies of Pluto and Mars ruled Scorpio.** Here Luna is in her Watery Deep Soul … she longs to come into Oneness. How can these energies help you activate more VIBRANT HEALTH … more Wholeness?

Darling Heart, we invite you to spend some quiet time on Sunday tuning into your beautiful SoulHeart, feeling into your dreams and wishes around your Health. Call on Archangel Raphael, the Angel of Scorpio, Angel of Healing, Love and Forgiveness to help you as you create more Vibrant Health!

And now, Sweet One, ask yourself the following question:

On a scale of 1 – 10 what's your number? _____
(10 is absolutely perfect vibrant health, 1 is being treated for illness)

And now, come to stillness and feel into your relationship with Your Health. Here are some common questions associated with Health. Check those that apply:

How often are you moving your body? (yoga, tai chi, qigong, running, walking, gym exercise, etc.)
1x week_____ 3x week_____ more than 3x week_____ I'm inconsistent_____ not at all _____
Are you eating foods to keep you vibrant? yes _____ no_____
Are you underweight? _____ overweight?_____
Do you meditate? 1x week_____ 3x week___ more than 3x week___ I'm inconsistent___ not at all ___
Are you sleeping well? yes _____ no ___ sometimes _____
How much time do you spend on your screen/devices daily? minutes _____ hours_____
Are you balancing work and play/family/friends? yes_____ no_____
Are you leaking energy by holding on to anger, blame, disappointment or loss? yes _____ no_____
Are you holding on to guilt? yes _____ no_____

From the questions above write down 3 possibilities where you can create even more VIBRANT HEALTH.

_____
_____
_____

Read each possibility out loud. Feel into them. Does one stand out from the other two? Does one bring a smile as you read it? Is one easier to manifest? Or do you feel the timing is right… Or not?

Which possibility on your list of 3 is the one to activate during this lunar cycle?

_____

NOVEMBER 15 SCORPIO NEW MOON CEREMONY OF CREATION

Gather Your Sacred Tools:

- The Angel Code Oracle 2020
- A candle and lighter
- Paper, pens, markers etc.
- A pen or pencil

Sweet One, go to a space where you won't be disturbed and light your candle. Call in Archangel Raphael to help inspire you as you come fully into your shining heart preparing to activate your New Moon dream! Allow yourself plenty of time to play with this!

Review the possibility you decided to activate during this lunar cycle and write a creation statement (an intention) to activate more VIBRANT HEALTH. Remember your statement is to be in the present and not in the future!

_____

OK, Dear Heart, now let's turn that intention into a goal with 3 actionable steps!

3 actions I am taking in the next two weeks to manifest more VIBRANT HEALTH!

_____

_____

_____

Awesome! You now have a goal and 3 actionable steps to take!

Here's the next part of your New Moon Creation Ceremony! We invite you to create a mini angel board! It's a vision board with the Angels! On your paper using your pens and markers write your intention and the 3 actions you are taking in the next two weeks!

Be sure to write Thank You on your board. You can write a simple Thank You or something more elaborate, "Thank You Angels and Lady Luna for this and all deliciousness I'm creating now!"

Be creative! Create something you'd like to look at least once a day, each and EVERY day! Make it fun … catchy … playful!!

When you've completed your mini angel board put your tools away.

Thank Archangel Raphael and Lady Luna and extinguish your candle.

Be sure to place your Angel Board where you will see it every day for the next two weeks!

Here are some things you might like to do to keep your mini angel board in your awareness:

- Take a picture on your phone and make it your screen saver.
- Take a photo on your computer and make it your screen saver.
- Frame it and put it on your desk or in your kitchen.
- Keep it on your bed stand. It's great seeing it first thing in the morning and again just before falling asleep!

Dear Heart, FOLLOW YOUR ACTIONABLE STEPS! When you DO something toward your goals you are actually creating an energetic alignment. And you know alignment helps you manifest more quickly!

NOV

november

S	M	T	W	T	F	S
1	2	3	4	5	6	7
8	9	10	11	12	13	14
15	16	17	18	19	20	21
22	23	24	25	26	27	28
29	30					

notes

9 MONDAY	**10** TUESDAY	**11** WEDNESDAY

12 THURSDAY	**13** FRIDAY	**14** SATURDAY	**15** SUNDAY
			NEW MOON ASTRO SIGN: SCORPIO ANGEL CODES: 12/5

NOV

november

S	M	T	W	T	F	S
1	2	3	4	5	6	7
8	9	10	11	12	13	14
15	16	17	18	19	20	21
22	23	24	25	26	27	28
29	30					

notes

16
MONDAY

17
TUESDAY

18
WEDNESDAY

19	20	21	22
THURSDAY	FRIDAY	SATURDAY	SUNDAY

NOV
november

S	M	T	W	T	F	S
1	2	3	4	5	6	7
8	9	10	11	12	13	14
15	16	17	18	19	20	21
22	23	24	25	26	27	28
29	30					

notes

23 MONDAY	24 TUESDAY	25 WEDNESDAY

26 THURSDAY	27 FRIDAY	28 SATURDAY	29 SUNDAY

November Full Moon Lunar Eclipse

DATE: MONDAY, NOVEMBER 30 / LUNATION: 4:32 AM (NEW YORK)
ASTRO SIGN: 8° GEMINI / RULER: MERCURY
ELEMENT: AIR / EXPRESSION: MUTABLE
ARCHANGEL: GABRIEL

FULL MOON KEY WORDS: COMPLETION, SURRENDER

ECLIPSES

This penumbral Lunar Eclipse is the fifth eclipse of the year. Eclipses usually come in pairs and activate a particular axis (astrological signs that are opposite each other). This eclipse in the sign of Gemini activates the Gemini/Sagittarius Axis. Eclipses amplify the lunar energies about three times more than a non-eclipse moon!

LUNA'S ASTRO ENERGIES

When Lady Luna comes to fullness in her Gemini frequencies she's asking, "What keeps you from being the toast of the town?" Have you been in your head? Researching … writing? Time to turn off the electronics, put on your favorite goddess garb and dancin' shoes and do some big-time socializing!

NOVEMBER 30 GEMINI FULL MOON ANGEL CODE 9/8

OVERLIGHTING ANGEL CODE 9 | GATEWAY OF DIVINE BLESSINGS
Activation: Activates your soul gifts and communication with benevolent Cosmic Beings; Angels, Star Beings and Unseen Guides.

This angel code is the energetic signature that awakens your soul gifts and opens your communication to all angels, star beings and guides throughout the cosmos.

ARCHANGEL ARIEL'S MESSAGE 9 | GATEWAY OF DIVINE BLESSINGS

Dear One, you are a Divine Being of Spirit. We are reminding you that you are Awakening to your Soul Gifts. You have many Soul Gifts; some are known to you and some are not. As you awaken your gifts you can communicate with Angels, Star Beings and Guides throughout the Cosmos. These benevolent beings are here awaiting your invitation to join you on your Earth journey.

LUNATION ANGEL CODE 8 | GATEWAY OF INFINITE POSSIBILITIES
Activation: Activates your limitless possibilities. Life on Earth is meant to be lived with infinite abundance!

This code is an Infinity Code connecting you to your Infinite Soul, nourishing and replenishing you with the Light of Infinite Possibilities. When this light flows through you, you can access your Soul Experiences. And, of course, the Sun is also activating 8!

ARCHANGEL ARIEL'S MESSAGE 8 | GATEWAY OF INFINITE POSSIBILITIES

You, Dear One, are a Divine Being holding the light of infinite possibilities. When you chose to incarnate on planet Earth you chose to experience all the delights this magical blue planet has to offer ... creating an abundant, joyful, vibrantly healthy, loving life for yourself! As a cosmic soul you were aware only of limitless, infinite possibility. We invite you to return to knowing that there are no limits and your life is truly filled with infinite possibilities awaiting you to choose the ones to activate!

NOVEMBER 30 GEMINI FULL MOON ACTIVATION FOR MATERIAL WEALTH

Full Moon activates completion and surrendering things in your life that no longer serve you. And, of course Dear One, always surrender with love and gratitude. This Full Moon you have the powerful support of Archangel Gabriel and Lady Luna in her Gemini energies as you're invited for the fourth time this year to surrender blocks to Material Wealth!

Please take some quiet time this week feeling into the **Angel Codes 9 | Gateway Of Divine Blessings** and **8 | Gateway Of Infinite Possibilities**. Feel into **Lady Luna's Astro Energies of Mercury ruled Gemini.** Here Luna flies through the Cosmos chatting and networking with everyone she sees. Her quicksilver mind comes up with all sorts of creative ideas! How can you use these energies to help you surrender blocks to Material Wealth?

Darling Heart, we invite you to spend some quiet time on Monday tuning into your beautiful Infinite Heart, feeling into your dreams and wishes. Feeling into Material Wealth. On this Full Moon decide on one thing you want to surrender that you believe is keeping you from experiencing an abundance of Material Wealth. To help you sort it out, call on Archangel Gabriel, Angel of Gemini, Angel of Divine Inspiration and Messages! Here's our checklist:

Material Wealth
On a scale of 1 – 10, what's your number? _____
(10 feeling absolutely divinely Wealthy, 1 wondering how you are going to pay your bills.)

Darling Heart, come to stillness and feel into your relationship with Money. Here are some common thoughts associated with money. Check those that apply.

How I Feel About My Money

I love having enough money to do all the things I love without ever having to think about how much it cost. _____

I just don't have enough for lot of extras. ____

I get a knot in my belly/ heart rate shifts when I think about money. __

Savings

I pay my savings account first. _____

I put money in my savings account every week/paycheck/month. ____

I have a retirement plan. ____

I don't have a solid plan. __

I live from paycheck to paycheck. ____

Purchases

I love new clothes and buy cute things when I see them.____

I can afford the things I want (gym/classes/conferences/vacations/travel). __

I rarely buy anything new. _____

Credit Cards

I use my charge accounts and pay them off every month. ____

I use my charge accounts and carry a balance. _____

I use my charge cards and pay the minimum each month. ____

Look at what you've checked and name one thing you are willing to surrender this Full Moon that you believe blocks your MATERIAL WEALTH.

_____

GEMINI FULL MOON FIRE CEREMONY OF SURRENDER

Gather Your Sacred Tools:

- 🕊 The Angel Code Oracle 2020
- 🕊 A candle and lighter
- 🕊 A fireproof bowl
- 🕊 A small piece of paper for burning
- 🕊 A pen or pencil

Sweet One, go to a space where you won't be disturbed and light your candle. Call in Archangel Gabriel to help you come fully into your shining heart as you release with love and gratitude. Write whatever you are surrendering on a small slip of paper and call on. Read what you've written out loud. You might use these words:

"By the light of this full moon I surrender _____to the Sacred Fires. I surrender with Love and Gratitude and I am now complete with _____."

Then light your paper and watch it burn. Knowing you have surrendered, released and are now complete. Sit for a moment. Feel into the power of surrender. And now write whatever impressions, feelings and awareness you have. _____
_____
_____
_____
_____

Thank Archangel Gabriel and Lady Luna and extinguish your fire.

What to do with the ashes? Many people choose to bury them. I like to go outside by the light of the moon, hold the ashes in my palm and blow them away!

Darling Heart, a surrendering ceremony is really powerful…trust that whatever you have released no longer has power over you and be sure not to re-invoke it into your life!

NOV

november

S	M	T	W	T	F	S
1	2	3	4	5	6	7
8	9	10	11	12	13	14
15	16	17	18	19	20	21
22	23	24	25	26	27	28
29	30					

notes

30 MONDAY	**1** TUESDAY	**2** WEDNESDAY
FULL MOON *PENUMBRAL LUNAR ECLIPSE* ASTRO SIGN: GEMINI ANGEL CODES: 9/8		

3 THURSDAY	**4** FRIDAY	**5** SATURDAY	**6** SUNDAY

December 2020 Overlighting Angel Code
7 | Gateway to The Divine Collective

Activation: Activates your connection to the Collective Consciousness.

December brings us the Overlighting Angel Code of 7, the energetic signature of Divine Collective Consciousness! Here, you are reminded that you are a being of Divine Energy. You are part of the Divine Collective. Your thoughts and actions are energy forms that affect the whole of life ... even the weather!

ARCHANGEL ARIEL'S MESSAGE 7 | GATEWAY TO THE DIVINE COLLECTIVE

Dear One, we invite you to awaken to the knowledge that All Are One. There is a collective ... no separation. You are part of the Whole. What you do, what you say, and what you think affects the Whole of Life... not just beings who breathe but the mountains, seas, waters, weather. All are a reflection of the energetic signature sent forth. Do you believe the words you speak are just words? Or do you understand the power they hold? You are a powerful creator! Once you breathe life into your words by speaking them aloud you have set a powerful invocation. You have released the energetic signature of those words into the universe. And the energy will build as it gathers more energy that is in vibrational coherence with its energetic signatures. Dear One, by the words you speak you can create Peace, Love, Kindness and Happiness in the collective or you can create War, Destruction, Disease and Divisiveness. What you create affects the whole of humanity. Keep your thoughts uplifted. Treat others with respect. Care for your planet. Understand All Are One and YOU affect the Whole! Now that you hold this understanding, we know you will create from your Divine SoulHeart.

DECEMBER ANGEL MANTRA

🕊 *"I am part of the Divine Collective. I choose words and actions that bring love, peace and kindness into the world."*

THIS MONTH'S ANGEL MANTRA ACTIVATION

Each morning, look into a mirror, begin taking long, slow, deep breaths all the way into your belly. As you breathe bring your awareness into your SoulHeart. Feel your beautiful SoulHeart expanding. Feel the shift. Do you feel warm... or cool? Do you feel vibration? See color? Now, bring your awareness back to your breath and take 3 long, slow, deep breaths. On each outbreath, repeat or tone the Angel Mantra out loud.

🕊 *"I am part of the Divine Collective. I choose words and actions that bring love, peace and kindness into the world."*

Repeat for a total of 3 breaths. For an even deeper alignment, repeat this in the evenings too!

december

SUNDAY	MONDAY	TUESDAY
		1
6	7	8
13	14 NEW MOON ECLIPSE (SAGITTARIUS) ANGEL CODES: 12/5	15
20	21 SOLSTICE	22
27	28	29 FULL MOON (CANCER) ANGEL CODES: 9/8

2020

WEDNESDAY	THURSDAY	FRIDAY	SATURDAY
2	3	4	5
9	10	11	12
16	17	18	19
23	24	25	26
30	31		

DEC
december

S	M	T	W	T	F	S
		1	2	3	4	5
6	7	8	9	10	11	12
13	14	15	16	17	18	19
20	21	22	23	24	25	26
27	28	29	30	31		

notes

7
MONDAY

8
TUESDAY

9
WEDNESDAY

10 THURSDAY	**11** FRIDAY	**12** SATURDAY	**13** SUNDAY

December New Moon Solar Eclipse

DATE: MONDAY, DECEMBER 14 / LUNATION: 11:18 AM (NEW YORK)
ASTRO SIGN: 23° SAGITTARIUS / RULER: JUPITER
ELEMENT: FIRE / EXPRESSION: MUTABLE
ARCHANGEL: URIEL

NEW MOON KEYWORDS: NEW BEGINNINGS, CREATION

ECLIPSES

Our sixth and final eclipse of 2020 is a total Solar Eclipse. Eclipses usually come in pairs and activate a particular axis (astrological signs that are opposite each other). This eclipse is the second eclipse this year in the sign of Sagittarius and activates the Gemini/Sagittarius Axis. Eclipses amplify the lunar energies about three times more than a non-eclipse moon!

LUNA'S ASTRO ENERGIES

Lady Luna brings this New Moon Solar Eclipse in Jupiter ruled Sagittarius, the happiest sign in the zodiac! When Luna shines her Sagittarian light, she is generous, idealistic and open-minded. She loves her freedom, the wind in her hair and exploring new places! During this portal of creation, you're being invited to create bountiful happiness knowing that the Universe will always provide!

DECEMBER 14 SAGITTARIUS NEW MOON SOLAR ECLIPSE ANGEL CODE 12/5

OVERLIGHTING ANGEL CODE 12 | GATEWAY TO THE HEART OF THE DIVINE MOTHER
Activation: Activates direct connection to the Divine through the Divine Mother Essence.

This Angel code activates direct connection to the divine through the Divine Mother essence.

ARCHANGEL ARIEL'S MESSAGE 12 | GATEWAY TO THE HEART OF THE DIVINE MOTHER

Here we have the energetic signature of the Divine Mother ... the essence of divinity of The All ... of God, Goddess, Creator, Source, however you understand THE ONE. Understand this energy, not as a mother you have known in physical form, but as a Divine Mother who comes in with the energetic signature of the Divine Creator and invites you to be open to the qualities of the Divine Feminine ... to understand that your world must now live through the SoulHeart. To live the qualities of the empowered mother ... of divine feminine .... Those qualities of unconditional love ... of honoring ... cooperation ... respect ... and allowing others to be what they are meant to be ... to live their lives following their own paths ... and to live your earth journey in your way ... knowing that you are a multidimensional Divine Spiritual Being. Through the frequencies of the Divine Mother essence you are also connected to all essences of the divine ... you are one with Divine Energy.

LUNATION ANGEL CODE 5 | GATEWAY TO THE ANGELIC TRIANGLE
Activation: Activates your connection to direct angel communication through the Angelic Triangle.

* To activate The Angelic Triangle, place your thumbs on your throat and your fingers on your ears. Do you feel the Triangle? Be still. Is there a Truth you need to speak? Is there a message you need to hear?

Darling Heart the angels reminding you to call on them. They are there for you so invite them into your life! And, of course, the Sun is also activating the 5!

ARCHANGEL ARIEL'S MESSAGE 5 | GATEWAY TO THE ANGELIC TRIANGLE

Dear One, you are always connected to the Angelic Realm. From the very beginning of all your beginnings you have had angels by your side. They are here for guidance and to share truths. Your angels cannot participate in your life without an invitation. Ask your angels to play with you ... to partner with you ... to offer guidance ... to share truths. Just as we do here with Little One, who you know as Beloved. Each morning when you awaken from slumber invite your angels to play with you!

DECEMBER 14 SAGITTARIUS NEW MOON ACTIVATION FOR MATERIAL WEALTH

New Moon activates new beginnings, visioning, setting goals and creating while you have the powerful support of Archangel Uriel and Lady Luna. On the last Full Moon, you were invited to surrender something that blocks your MATERIAL WEALTH so now, on this New Moon, we invite you, for the fourth time, to create more wealth in your life!

As we move through the Wheel of the Year, this New Moon is the fourth time we are inviting you to manifest MATERIAL WEALTH!

Please take some quiet time this week feeling into the **Angel Codes 12 | Gateway To The Heart of The Divine Mother** and **5 | Gateway To The Angelic Triangle**. Feel into the **Lady Luna's Astro**

Energies of Jupiter ruled Sagittarius. Here Luna is on Fire and ready to ignite your dreams! Riding tandem with beneficent Jupiter it's time to create BIG!!! How can these energies help you create more MATERIAL WEALTH?

Darling Heart, we invite you to spend some quiet time on Sunday tuning into your beautiful Infinite Heart, feeling into your dreams and wishes around your Wealth. Call on Archangel Uriel, Angel of Sagittarius, Angel of Light and Clarity to help you clarify the change you are making as you create more MATERIAL WEALTH!

Sweet One, ask yourself the following question:

Material Wealth
On a scale of 1 – 10 what's your number? _____
(10 feeling absolutely divinely wealthy, 1 wondering how you are going to pay your bills.)

Darling Heart, come to stillness and feel into your relationship with Money. Here are some common thoughts associated with money. Check those that apply:

How I Feel About My Money
I love having enough money to do all the things I love without ever having to think about
    how much it cost. _____
I just don't have enough lots of extras. ____
I get a knot in my belly/ heart rate shifts when I think about money. ____

Savings
I pay my savings account first. _____
I put money in my savings account every week/paycheck/month. _____
I have a retirement plan. ____
I don't have a solid plan. __
I live from paycheck to paycheck. ____

Purchases
I love new clothes and buy cute things when I see them._____
I can afford the things I want (gym/classes/conferences/vacations/travel).__
I rarely buy anything new._____

Credit Cards
I use my charge accounts and pay them off every month. _____
I use my charge accounts and carry a balance. _____

I use my charge cards and pay the minimum each month. ____

From the list above write down 3 possible ways you can create more MATERIAL WEALTH.

_____

_____

_____

Which possibility on your list of 3 is the one to activate during this lunar cycle?

_____

DECEMBER 14 SAGITTARIUS NEW MOON CEREMONY OF CREATION

Gather Your Sacred Tools:

- A candle and lighter
- Paper, pens, markers etc.
- The Angel Code Oracle 2020
- A pen or pencil

Sweet One, go to a space where you won't be disturbed and light your candle. Call in Archangel Uriel to help inspire you as you come fully into your shining heart preparing to activate your New Moon dream! Allow yourself plenty of time to play with this!

Review the possibility you decided to activate during this lunar cycle and write a creation statement (an intention) to activate more Material Wealth. Remember your statement is to be in the present and not in the future!

_____

OK, Dear Heart, now let's turn that intention into a goal with 3 actionable steps!

3 Actions I am taking in the next two weeks to manifest more MATERIAL WEALTH!

_____

_____

_____

Awesome! You now have a goal and 3 actionable steps to take!
Here's the next part of your New Moon Creation Ceremony! We invite you to create a mini angel board! It's a vision board with the Angels! On your paper using your pens and markers write your intention and the 3 actions you are taking in the next two weeks!

Be sure to write Thank You on your board. You can write a simple Thank You or something more elaborate, "Thank You Angels and Lady Luna for this and all deliciousness I'm creating now!"

Be creative! Create something you'd like to look at least once a day, each and EVERY day! Make it fun … catchy … playful!!

When you've completed your mini angel board put your tools away.

Thank Archangel Uriel and Lady Luna and extinguish your candle.

Be sure to place your Angel Board where you will see it every day for the next two weeks!

Here are some things you might like to do to keep your mini angel board in your awareness:

- Take a picture on your phone and make it your screen saver.
- Take a photo on your computer and make it your screen saver.
- Frame it and put it on your desk or in your kitchen.
- Keep it on your bed stand. It's great seeing it first thing in the morning and again just before falling asleep!

Dear Heart, FOLLOW YOUR ACTIONABLE STEPS! When you DO something toward your goals you are actually creating an energetic alignment. And you know alignment helps you manifest more quickly!

DEC
december

S	M	T	W	T	F	S
		1	2	3	4	5
6	7	8	9	10	11	12
13	14	15	16	17	18	19
20	21	22	23	24	25	26
27	28	29	30	31		

notes

14
MONDAY

15
TUESDAY

16
WEDNESDAY

NEW MOON

TOTAL SOLAR ECLIPSE

ASTRO SIGN:
SAGITTARIUS

ANGEL CODES: 12/5

17 THURSDAY	**18** FRIDAY	**19** SATURDAY	**20** SUNDAY

DEC
december

S	M	T	W	T	F	S
		1	2	3	4	5
6	7	8	9	10	11	12
13	14	15	16	17	18	19
20	21	22	23	24	25	26
27	28	29	30	31		

notes

21 MONDAY	**22** TUESDAY	**23** WEDNESDAY
SOLSTICE		

24 THURSDAY	25 FRIDAY	26 SATURDAY	27 SUNDAY

December Full Moon

DATE: TUESDAY, DECEMBER 29 / LUNATION: 10:30 PM (NEW YORK)
ASTRO SIGN: 8° CANCER / RULER: MOON
ELEMENT: WATER / EXPRESSION: CARDINAL
ARCHANGEL: RAPHAEL

FULL MOON KEYWORDS: COMPLETION, SURRENDER

LUNA ASTRO ENERGIES

When Lady Luna is shining her Cancerian light, she is highlighting home and family. We invite you to tune into your Infinite Heart. Where does your beautiful SoulHeart feel "at home"? Who is your Heart family? Time to surrender anything that keeps your Infinite Heart from feeling LOVED!

DECEMBER 29 CANCER FULL MOON ANGEL CODE 9/8

OVERLIGHTING ANGEL CODE 9 | GATEWAY OF DIVINE BLESSINGS
Activation: Activates your soul gifts and communication with benevolent Cosmic Beings; Angels, Star Beings and Unseen Guides.

This angel code is the energetic signature that awakens your soul gifts and opens your communications to all angels, star beings and guides throughout the cosmos.

ARCHANGEL ARIELS MESSAGE 9 | GATEWAY OF DIVINE BLESSINGS

Dear One, you are a divine being of spirit. You have many SOUL gifts; some are known to you and some are not. You have the ability to connect with all Angels, Star Beings and Guides throughout the cosmos. These benevolent beings are here awaiting your invitation to join you on your Earth journey.

LUNATION ANGEL CODE 8 | GATEWAY OF INFINITE POSSIBILITIES
Activation: Activates your limitless possibilities. Life on Earth is meant to be lived with infinite abundance!

The angels are inviting you to connect to your Infinite Soul, replenishing yourself as the Light of Infinite Possibilities flows through your entire system. When this light flows through you, you can access your Soul Experiences. This gateway is amplified by the Sun as it also activates 8!

ARCHANGEL ARIEL'S MESSAGE 8 | GATEWAY OF INFINITE POSSIBILITIES

You, Dear One, are a Divine Being holding the light of infinite possibilities. When you chose to incarnate on planet Earth you chose to experience all the delights this magical blue planet had to offer … creating an abundant, joyful, vibrantly healthy, loving life for yourself! As a cosmic soul you were aware only a limitless, infinite possibility. We invite you to return to that knowing. There are no limits and your life is truly filled with infinite possibilities awaiting you to choose the ones to activate!

DECEMBER 29 CANCER FULL MOON ACTIVATION FOR LOVE

What a magical year **2020 THE YEAR OF THE INFINITE HEART** has been! Full Moons activate completion and surrendering things in your life that no longer serve a purpose. And, of course, Sweet One, always surrender with love and gratitude!

We began the year with the January 10th Full Moon Eclipse where we had the powerful support of Archangel Raphael and Lady Luna in her Full Moon Cancerian energies. And, now, for this final Full Moon of 2020, as you surrender blocks to LOVE, you are again receiving powerful support from Archangel Raphael and Lady Luna in her Cancerian energies.

Take some quiet time this week feeling into the **Angel Codes 9 | Gateway Of Divine Blessings** and **8 | Gateway Of Infinite Possibilities.** Feel into **Lady Luna's Astro Energies of Moon ruled Cancer**. Here Luna is in the watery depth of her soul!! She longs for Oneness. How can you use these energies to help you surrender blocks to LOVE?

Darling Heart, we invite you to spend some quiet time on Tuesday tuning into your beautiful Infinite Heart, feeling into your dreams and wishes. Feeling into Love. On this Full Moon decide on one thing you want to surrender that you believe is keeping your Heart from experiencing its most delicious Joy. To help you sort it out, call on Archangel Raphael, Angel of Cancer, Angel of the Heart, Angel of Love, Healing and Forgiveness. For this final Full Moon of the year let's focus, again, on your beautiful Self! Here's a simple checklist:

What is your passion? _____
_____

What makes your heart sing? _____
_____

Do you have a BFF? yes ___no____
Are you in a meaningful relationship? yes__ no____

Are you close to your family? yes __ no__
Are you nourishing yourself? yes__ no__
If you checked no, what is keeping you from nourishing your beautiful self?

_____

_____

Do you feel good about who you are? yes__ no__ If you checked no, what don't you feel good about?

_____

_____

BONUS QUESTION
How much do you love yourself? What's your number? _____
On a scale of 1-10 (10 is *Yes! I'm absolutely totally awesome!* 1 is *I'm a mess. Totally unworthy of love.*)

If you rated yourself less than 10, what is keeping you from absolutely adoring your totally awesome
self? _____

Look at what you've written and name one thing you are willing to surrender this Full Moon to that
you believe blocks Love in your life.

_____

_____

DECEMBER 29 CANCER FULL MOON FIRE CEREMONY OF SURRENDER

Gather Your Sacred Tools:

- The Angel Code Oracle 2020
- A candle and lighter
- A fireproof bowl
- A small piece of paper for burning
- A pen or pencil

Go to a space where you won't be disturbed and light your candle. Call in Archangel Raphael to help
you come fully into your shining heart as you release with love and gratitude. Write whatever you are
surrendering on a small slip of paper. Read what you've written out loud. You might use these words.

"By the light of this full moon I surrender _____to the Sacred Fires.
I surrender with Love and Gratitude and I am now complete with _____."

Then light your paper and watch it burn. Knowing you have surrendered, released and are now complete. Sit for a moment. Feel into the power of surrender. And now write whatever impressions, feelings and awareness you have. _____

_____

_____

_____

_____

Thank Archangel Raphael and Lady Luna and extinguish your fire.

What to do with the ashes? Many people choose to bury them. I like to go outside by the light of the moon, hold the ashes in my palm and blow them away!

Darling Heart, a surrendering ceremony is really powerful…trust that whatever you have released no longer has power over you and be sure not to re-invoke it into your life!

Yoo-hoo! Angel Code Oracle 2021 is in production…

We're pleased to announce THE ANGEL CODE ORACLE 2021 is in production! Have you signed up for the waitlist, yet? It's easy. Just send an e-mail to:
Taco2021waitlist@katebeloved.com

We'll send an e-mail as soon as it's available!

We know you're creating an amazing year!
Abundant Angel Blessings
Beloveds

DEC

december

S	M	T	W	T	F	S
		1	2	3	4	5
6	7	8	9	10	11	12
13	14	15	16	17	18	19
20	21	22	23	24	25	26
27	28	29	30	31		

notes

28
MONDAY

29
TUESDAY

FULL MOON

ASTRO SIGN: CANCER

ANGEL CODES: 9/8

30
WEDNESDAY

31 THURSDAY	1 FRIDAY	2 SATURDAY	3 SUNDAY

Yoo-Hoo! You Did It!

Blessings Darling Heart,

Yoo-Hoo! You've done it! You've spent 2020 partnering with the angels, aligning with the lunar cycles, clarifying your dreams, setting goals, releasing what no longer serves you and creating a more delicious life! You are amazing!

We hope you're continuing your journey with us through 2021 with our next playbook THE ANGEL CODE ORACLE 2021; A 12-Month Journey Activating The Angelic Gateway!

Thank you so much for taking this journey with us.
Wishing you an absolutely magical 2021. May your heart be filled to overflowing and may you awaken each and every one you meet.

Abundant Angel Blessings
Beloved

To learn more about our work and how we can help you continue to transform your life please visit us at www.KateBeloved.com You'll even find some awesome freebies.